Contents

Introduction

Whimsical or geometric, traditional or contemporary, for the bed, table, or wall, for kids, for guys, or for yourself, *Quiltmaker* foundation-pieced patterns cover a broad spectrum of styles and uses. This collection of quilts takes you through the seasons with happy spring colors, bright summer flowers, comforting fall fun, cozy winter ideas, and holiday projects that are sure to inspire you throughout the year.

Foundation piecing is a terrific technique for patches that are small or unusually shaped. There are simple designs if you're new to foundation piecing ("Noah's Arks," page 62) and challenging projects if you're more confident ("Great Ball of Fire," page 46). If you can quilt a straight line, you can make the quilts in this book. See "Foundation-Piecing Basics" (page 86) for a helpful lesson in foundation piecing.

Whether you're shopping for new fabrics or selecting from your stash, you can add a personal touch to each pattern with the colors you love. You'll find color options for most of the quilts presented in this book to help you see beyond the featured quilt. Look at the designs and imagine your own color schemes.

Many quiltmakers finish a quilt top, and then feel stuck because they don't know how to quilt it. You'll find a quilting suggestion for every project in this book to help you finish your quilt beautifully.

Enjoy!

June Dudley
Editor-in-Chief
Quiltmaker
quiltmaker.com

Foundation-Pieced Quilts

14 Favorites from
Quiltmaker Magazine

Foundation-Pieced Quilts: 14 Favorites from *Quiltmaker* Magazine
© 2011 from the Editors of *Quiltmaker* Magazine

The Quilts You Want to Make—We Show You How

That Patchwork Place® is an imprint of Martingale & Company®.

Martingale & Company
19021 120th Ave. NE, Suite 102
Bothell, WA 98011-9511 USA
www.martingale-pub.com

Credits

President & CEO: Tom Wierzbicki

Editor in Chief: Mary V. Green

Managing Editor: Karen Costello Soltys

Design Director: Stan Green

Production Manager: Regina Girard

Technical Editor: Nancy Mahoney

Copy Editor: Marcy Heffernan

Illustrator: Laurel Strand

Cover & Text Designer: Stan Green

Photography provided by Mellisa Karlin Mahoney, Brent Kane, and Joe Hancock Studio (pages 5, 9, 16, 27, 51, and 56)

Quiltmaker, ISSN 1047-1634, is published bimonthly by Creative Crafts Group, LLC, 741 Corporate Circle, Suite A, Golden, CO 80401, www.quiltmaker.com.

Printed in China
16 15 14 13 12 11   8 7 6 5 4 3 2 1

Library of Congress Cataloging-in-Publication Data is available upon request.

ISBN: 978-1-60468-135-2

Mission Statement

Dedicated to providing quality products and service
to inspire creativity.

Bahama Breeze

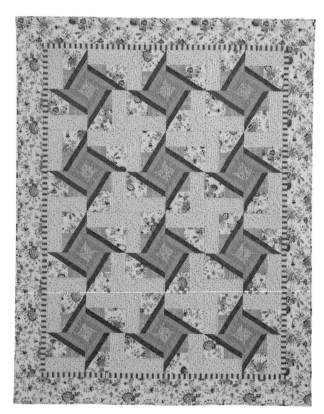

Designed by Jean Paul Dugas; made by Peg Spradlin

Finished Quilt: 60½" x 76½"
Finished Blocks: 16"

Materials

- Light green floral, 3 yards for blocks, outer border, and binding
- Light yellow print, 1⅓ yards for blocks
- Dark teal tone-on-tone fabric, 1 yard for blocks
- Medium teal print, 1 yard for blocks
- Orange print, ⅝ yard for blocks
- Green tone-on-tone fabric, ½ yard for blocks
- Multicolored striped fabric, ½ yard for inner border
- Green-and-teal print, ⅓ yard for blocks
- Backing, 5 yards
- Batting, 68" x 84"

Note: Although yardage amounts for foundation piecing are adequate, you may need more if you cut very generous pieces.

Cutting

From the light yellow print, cut:
  48 rectangles, 3½" x 8½"

From the multicolored striped fabric, cut:
  7 inner-border strips, 1½" x 42"

From the *lengthwise* grain of the light green floral, cut:
  2 outer-border strips, 5½" x 69"
  2 outer-border strips, 5½" x 63"
  5 binding strips, 2¼" x 59"

Making the Blocks

Refer to "Foundation-Piecing Basics" on page 86 for detailed instructions as needed.

1. Make 48 copies of the foundation pattern on page 8.

2. Paper piece the units in numerical order in the colors indicated on the pattern. Press and trim after adding each piece.

Make 48.

3. Noting the orientation, sew a yellow rectangle to each foundation-pieced unit. Press the seam allowances toward the yellow rectangles.

4. Sew together four units from step 3 as shown to make a block. Repeat to make a total of 12 blocks.

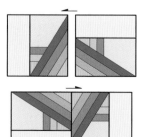

Make 12.

Assembling the Quilt

1. Join the blocks in four rows of three blocks each. Press the seam allowances in opposite directions from row to row. Sew the rows together and press the seam allowances in one direction.

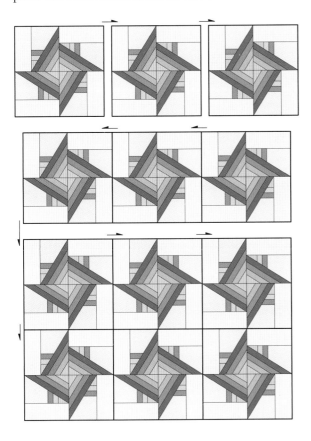

2. Sew the multicolored striped strips together end to end to make a continuous strip. Cut two 64½"-long strips for the side inner borders and two 50½"-long strips for the top and bottom inner borders.

3. Sew the side border strips to the quilt and press the seam allowances toward the borders. Add the top and bottom border strips in the same manner.

4. Referring to "Squared Borders" on page 92, measure, cut, and sew the 69"-long light green floral outer-border strips to the sides of the quilt top. Then add the 63"-long light green floral outer-border strips to the top and bottom of the quilt top. Press the seam allowances toward the just-added borders.

5. Remove the foundation papers.

Quilting and Finishing

1. Layer and baste together the backing, batting, and quilt top.

2. See the quilting suggestion below.

3. Bind the quilt using the 2¼"-wide light green floral strips.

Quilting Suggestion

Color Option

Eye of the Storm

Rotate just one quarter of each block 180° to create a star shape at the center in this version.

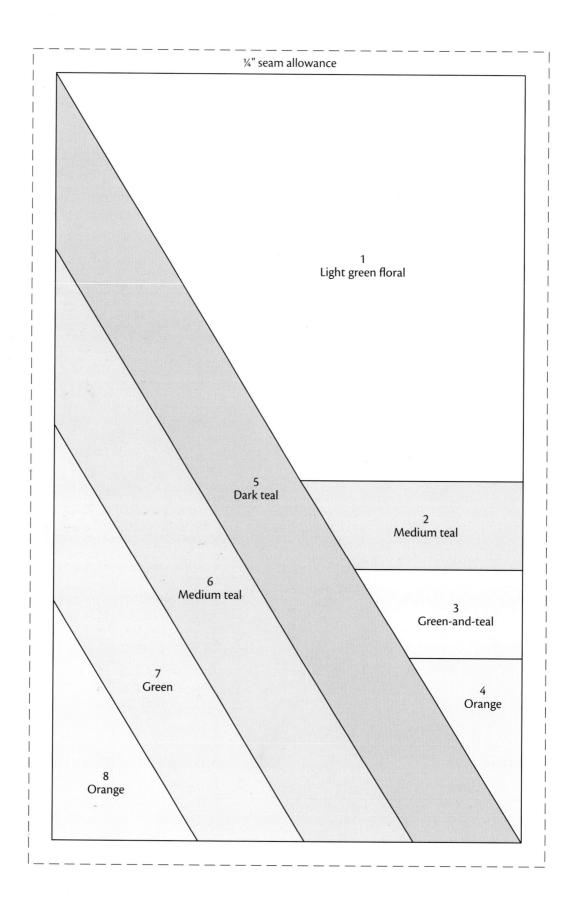

¼" seam allowance

1
Light green floral

5
Dark teal

2
Medium teal

6
Medium teal

3
Green-and-teal

7
Green

4
Orange

8
Orange

Dakota Snowstorm

Finished Quilt: 81½" x 99½"
Finished Blocks: 9"

Materials

- White tone-on-tone fabric, 7⅛ yards for blocks and binding
- Dark blue tone-on-tone fabric, 3⅞ yards for blocks
- Medium blue tone-on-tone fabric, 1¾ yards for blocks
- Light blue tone-on-tone fabric, 1½ yards for blocks
- Backing, 7⅞ yards
- Batting, 89" x 107"

Note: Although yardage amounts for foundation piecing are adequate, you may need more if you cut very generous pieces.

Cutting

From the white tone-on-tone fabric, cut:
10 binding strips, 2¼" x 42"
30 squares, 9½" x 9½"
32 rectangles, 5" x 9½"

From the dark blue tone-on-tone fabric, cut:
32 squares, 2¾" x 2¾"
48 squares, 3¼" x 3¼"; cut in half diagonally to yield 96 triangles

From the light blue tone-on-tone fabric, cut:
76 squares, 2¾" x 2¾"
58 squares, 3¼" x 3¼"; cut in half diagonally to yield 116 triangles

Designed by Jodi Crowell; sewn by Mickie Swall; quilted by Claudia Whitlock

Making the Blocks

Refer to "Foundation-Piecing Basics" on page 86 for detailed instructions as needed.

1. Mark a diagonal line from corner to corner on the wrong side of the 2¾" dark blue and light blue squares. Place a dark blue square on one corner of a 9½" white square, right sides together. Sew on the marked line and trim away the corner fabric, leaving a ¼" seam allowance. Flip the resulting triangle open and press the seam allowances toward the triangle. Make four of block T.

Block T.
Make 4.

2. Repeat step 1, sewing two dark blue squares and two light blue squares to a white square to make 14 of block W.

Block W.
Make 14.

3. Repeat step 1, sewing four light blue squares to each of the remaining white squares to make 12 of block Z.

Block Z.
Make 12.

4. Using the foundation patterns on pages 14 and 15, make 148 copies of unit A and 32 copies of unit B.

5. Paper piece 32 A units in numerical order in the colors indicated on the pattern, using the dark blue tone-on-tone triangles for piece 5. Press and trim after adding each piece.

Unit A.
Make 32.

6. Paper piece 116 A units in numerical order in the colors indicated on the pattern, using the light blue tone-on-tone triangles for piece 5. Press and trim after adding each piece.

Unit A.
Make 116.

7. Paper piece 32 B units in numerical order in the colors indicated on the pattern, using the dark blue triangles for pieces 6 and 7. Press and trim after adding each piece.

Unit B.
Make 32.

8. Sew a white rectangle to each B unit as shown to make 32 of block U. Press the seam allowances toward the rectangle.

Block U.
Make 32.

9. Noting the orientation of the units, lay out three A units with a dark blue corner and one A unit with a light blue corner as shown. Sew the units together to make block V; press. Make four of these blocks.

Block V.
Make 4.

10. Sew two A units with a dark blue corner and two A units with a light blue corner together as shown to make block X; press. Make 10 blocks.

Block X.
Make 10.

11. Sew four A units with a light blue corner together to make block Y; press. Make 23 blocks.

Block Y.
Make 23.

Assembling the Quilt

1. Paying careful attention to the block placement, lay out the blocks in 11 rows of nine blocks each as shown in the assembly diagram. Sew the blocks together into rows as indicated. Press the seam allowances in opposite directions from row to row.

2. Join the rows and press the seam allowances in one direction.

3. Remove the foundation papers.

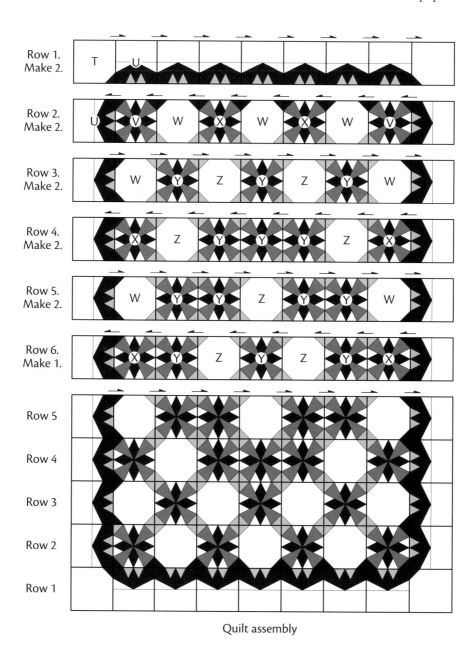

Quilt assembly

Quilting and Finishing

1. Layer and baste together the backing, batting, and quilt top.

2. See the quilting suggestion below.

3. Bind the quilt using the 2¼"-wide white tone-on-tone strips.

Quilting Suggestion

Dakota Embers

This variation uses only block Y, colored in two different ways. The complementary color scheme of red and green takes the design in a different direction.

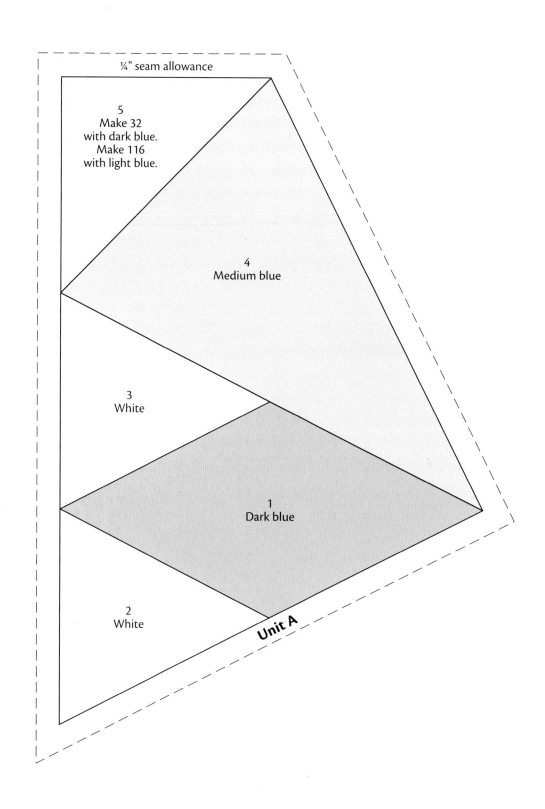

¼" seam allowance

5
Make 32
with dark blue.
Make 116
with light blue.

4
Medium blue

3
White

1
Dark blue

2
White

Unit A

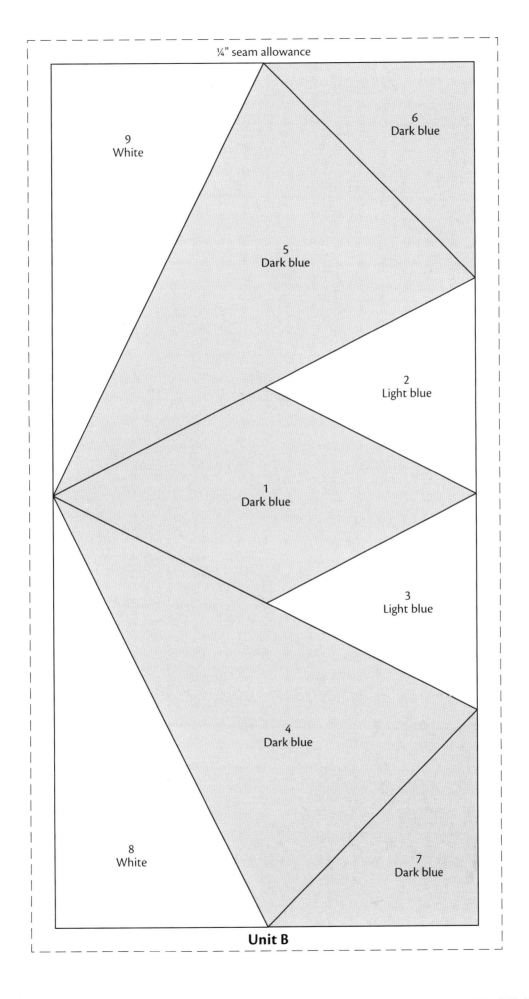

¼" seam allowance

9
White

6
Dark blue

5
Dark blue

2
Light blue

1
Dark blue

3
Light blue

4
Dark blue

8
White

7
Dark blue

Unit B

Evening at Home

About This Quilt

This quilt is deceptive—it looks as if it's made with two different Star blocks. The smaller stars are actually the result when the foundation-pieced sections are sewn together. Who would have guessed this foundation pattern could turn into such an interesting quilt?

Finished Quilt: 93½" x 93½"
Finished Blocks: 15"

Materials

- Green #1 print, 3 yards for blocks and outer border
- Gold print, 2½ yards for blocks and inner border
- Dark green tone-on-tone fabric, 2⅛ yards for blocks
- Red print, 2 yards for blocks and binding
- Light tan print, 2 yards for blocks
- Blue print, 1¾ yards for blocks
- Brown print, 1½ yards for blocks
- Green #2 print, ⅝ yard for blocks
- Backing, 9 yards
- Batting, 101" x 101"

Note: Although yardage amounts for foundation piecing are adequate, you may need more if you cut very generous pieces.

Cutting

From the *lengthwise* grain of the gold print, cut:
    2 inner-border strips, 3½" x 78"
    2 inner-border strips, 3½" x 84"
    25 squares, 3½" x 3½"

From the *lengthwise* grain of green print 1, cut:
    2 outer-border strips, 6½" x 84"
    2 outer-border strips, 6½" x 96"

From the red print, cut:
    11 binding strips, 2¼" x 42"

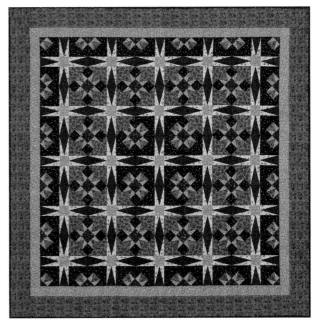

Designed by Joyce Robinson; sewn by Mickie Swall;
quilted by Lori King

Making the Blocks

Refer to "Foundation-Piecing Basics" on page 86 for detailed instructions as needed.

1. Make 100 copies of the foundation pattern on page 20.

2. Paper piece 48 units in numerical order in the colors indicated on the pattern, using the red print for piece 7. Press and trim after adding each piece.

Make 48.

3. Paper piece 52 units in numerical order in the colors indicated on the pattern, using the brown print for piece 7. Press and trim after adding each piece.

Make 52.

4. To make block W, sew a red unit from step 2 to a 3½" gold square, starting from the raw edges and stopping in the center of the square. Working in a counterclockwise direction, add a red unit, a brown unit from step 3, and then sew another red unit to the top as shown, and complete the partial seam. Press the seam allowances toward each newly added unit. Repeat to make a total of four blocks.

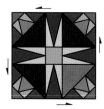

Block W.
Make 4.

5. In the same way, make the specified number of X, Y, and Z blocks using the indicated units and paying careful attention to color placement in each block.

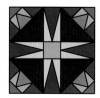

Block X.
Make 16.

Block Y.
Make 4.

Block Z.
Make 1.

Assembling the Quilt

1. Noting the placement and orientation of the blocks, refer to the assembly diagram and join the blocks to make the rows as indicated. Press the seam allowances in opposite directions from row to row. Sew the rows together and press the seam allowances in one direction.

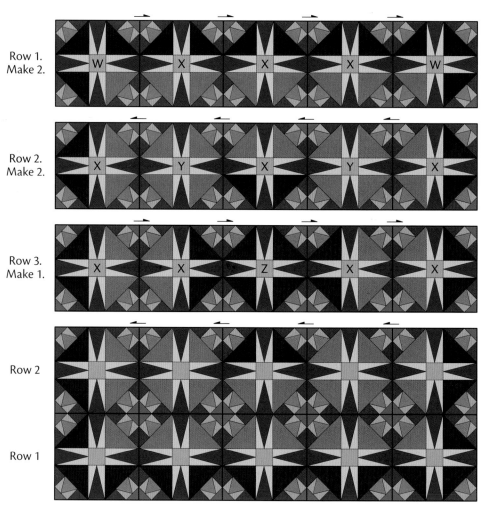

Row 1.
Make 2.

Row 2.
Make 2.

Row 3.
Make 1.

Row 2

Row 1

Quilt assembly

2. Referring to "Squared Borders" on page 92, measure, cut, and sew the 78"-long gold print inner-border strips to the sides of the quilt top. Then add the 84"-long gold inner-border strips to the top and bottom of the quilt top. Press the seam allowances toward the just-added borders.

3. In the same way, measure, cut, and sew the green #1 print outer-border strips to the sides and then the top and bottom of the quilt top.

4. Remove the foundation papers.

Quilting and Finishing

1. Layer and baste together the backing, batting, and quilt top.

2. See the quilting suggestion below.

3. Bind the quilt using the 2¼"-wide red print strips.

Country Style

This variation calls to mind a walk in the country with blue skies and green grass.

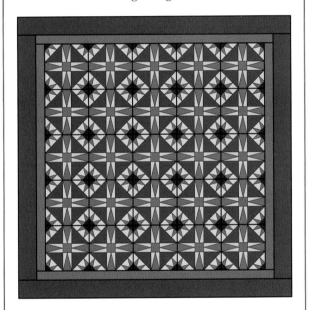

Quilting Suggestion

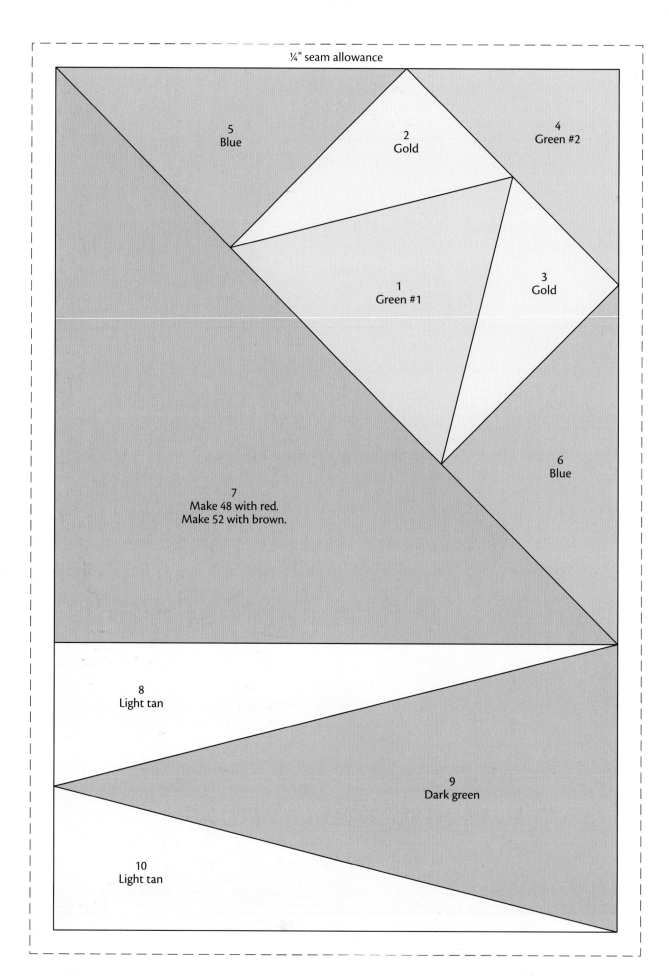

¼" seam allowance

5
Blue

2
Gold

4
Green #2

1
Green #1

3
Gold

6
Blue

7
Make 48 with red.
Make 52 with brown.

8
Light tan

9
Dark green

10
Light tan

Palm Star

Finished Quilt: 64¼" x 73½"
Finished Row Width: 8⅝"

Materials

- Red print, 1⅜ yards for units
- Dark pink print, 2⅛ yards for units and middle border
- Light pink print, 1⅜ yards for units
- Dark teal print, ⅝ yard for binding
- Medium teal print, 2⅛ yards for units
- Light teal print, ½ yard for inner border
- Teal multicolored print, 2½ yards for units and outer border
- Medium green print, 1¼ yards for units
- Medium-light green print, 3¼ yards for units
- Light green print, 5½ yards for units
- Green multicolored print, 1 yard for units
- White print, ¾ yard for units
- Backing, 4¾ yards
- Batting, 72" x 81"
- Water-soluble foundation paper (optional; see page 24)

Note: Although yardage amounts for foundation piecing are adequate, you may need more if you cut very generous pieces.

Rough and Ready

To conserve fabric and speed up the sewing process, we recommend cutting oversized pieces for foundation piecing. Make extra copies of the foundations, and then cut them apart to make a template for each piece, adding roughly ½" all around. Label each template with its piece number and color. Cut the strips in widths as indicated in the cutting list for each fabric. Place the templates right side up on the *wrong side* of the fabric and cut out the pieces. Refer to step 1 of "Making the Quilt Top" and the foundation patterns for piece quantities.

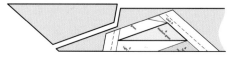

Cutting piece 4 in unit A

Designed by Debbie Reed; sewn by Penny Wolf; quilted by Carolee Miller

Cutting

The foundation patterns are on pages 25 and 26. Yardages were calculated based on precutting pieces from strips. Follow the tip "Rough and Ready" to prepare your pieces. Notice that foundation pieces are listed as numbers in the cutting list and correlate to the numbers on the foundation patterns.

From the red print, cut:
    2" x 42" strips (16, 23, 30, 31)

From the dark pink print, cut:
    7 middle-border strips, 1½" x 42"
    2¼" x 42" strips (20, 27, 38, 39)

From the light pink print, cut:
    2" x 42" strips (18, 25, 34, 35)

From the dark teal print, cut:
    8 binding strips, 2¼" x 42"

From the medium teal print, cut:
    2½" x 42" strips (21, 28, 40, 41)

From the light teal print, cut:
    7 inner-border strips, 1½" x 42"

From the *lengthwise* grain of the teal multicolored print, cut:

 2 outer-border strips, 4½" x 75"
 2 outer-border strips, 4½" x 67"
 2" x 75" strips (6, 13)

From the medium green print, cut:

 2" x 42" strips (4, 11)

From the medium-light green print, cut:

 2" x 42" strips (17, 19, 24, 26, 32, 33, 36, 37)

From the light green print, cut:

 2½" x 42" strips (1, 3, 5, 7, 8, 10, 12, 14)

From the green multicolored print, cut:

 2" x 42" strips (2, 9)

From the white print, cut:

 2½" x 42" strips (15, 22, 29)

Making the Quilt Top

Refer to "Foundation-Piecing Basics" on page 86 for detailed instructions as needed.

1. Make copies of the foundation patterns on pages 25 and 26 in the quantities listed below. Paper piece the units in numerical order in the colors indicated on the pattern. Press and trim after adding each piece.

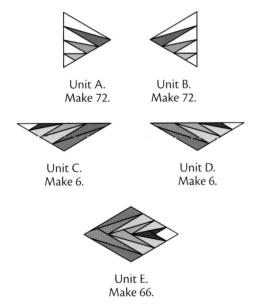

Unit A.
Make 72.

Unit B.
Make 72.

Unit C.
Make 6.

Unit D.
Make 6.

Unit E.
Make 66.

2. Join the units to make the sections as shown and press the seam allowances open.

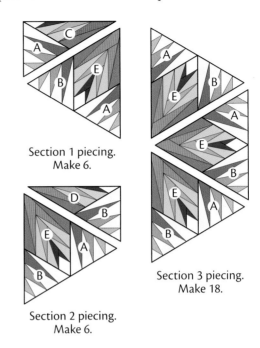

Section 1 piecing.
Make 6.

Section 2 piecing.
Make 6.

Section 3 piecing.
Make 18.

3. Join the sections to make vertical rows as indicated. Press the seam allowances open. Then sew the rows together and press.

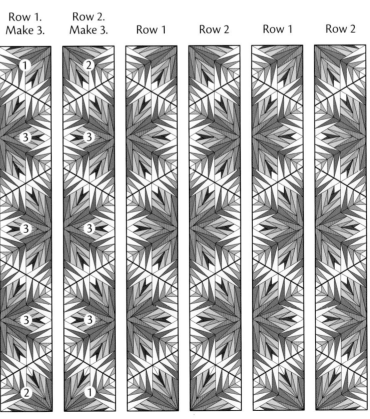

Row 1.
Make 3.

Row 2.
Make 3.

Row 1

Row 2

Row 1

Row 2

Quilt assembly

4. Sew the light teal inner-border strips together end to end to make a continuous strip. Cut this strip into two 65"-long strips for the side borders and two 57"-long strips for the top and bottom borders.

5. Sew the dark pink middle-border strips together end to end to make a continuous strip. Cut this strip into two 67"-long strips for the side borders and two 59"-long strips for the top and bottom borders.

6. Matching the centers, join the corresponding inner-, middle-, and outer-border strips to make four border units.

Border unit.
Make 4.

7. Referring to "Mitered Borders" on page 93, sew the border units to the quilt and miter the corners. Trim the seam allowances to ¼" and press them open.

8. Remove the foundation papers.

Quilting and Finishing

1. Layer and baste together the backing, batting, and quilt top.

2. See the quilting suggestion at upper right.

3. Bind the quilt using the 2¼"-wide dark teal strips.

Choosing Foundation Paper

With the many narrow points in this pattern, using water-soluble foundation paper will make removing the foundations easier.

Quilting Suggestion

Color Option

Let It Snow

To make a scrappy snowstorm, choose bright white and light blue prints to contrast with deep blues and indigos.

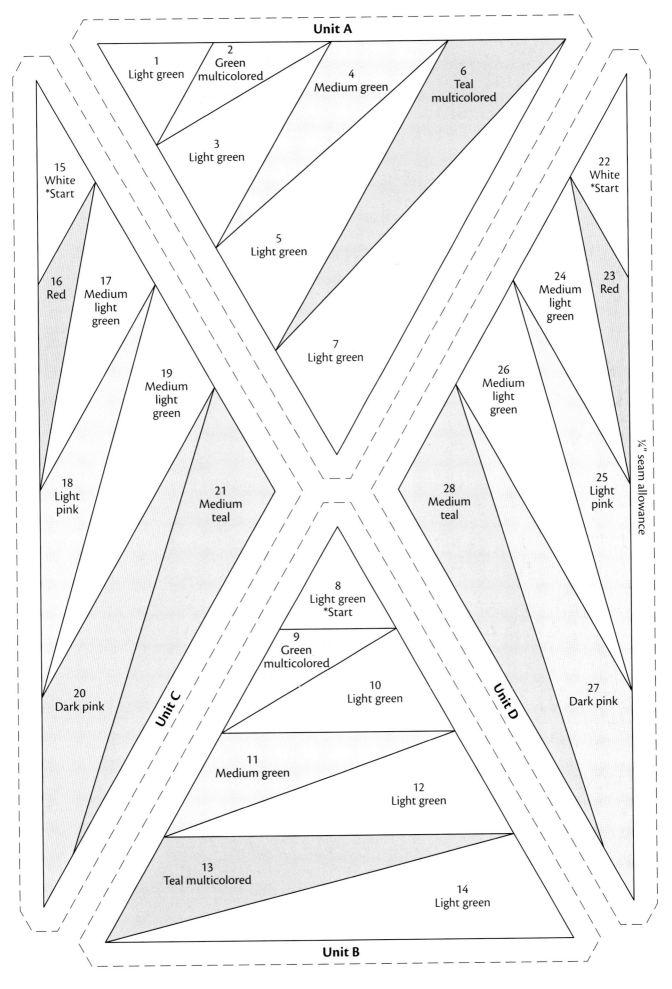

Unit A

1 Light green

2 Green multicolored

3 Light green

4 Medium green

6 Teal multicolored

5 Light green

7 Light green

15 White *Start

16 Red

17 Medium light green

18 Light pink

19 Medium light green

20 Dark pink

21 Medium teal

22 White *Start

23 Red

24 Medium light green

25 Light pink

26 Medium light green

27 Dark pink

28 Medium teal

8 Light green *Start

9 Green multicolored

10 Light green

11 Medium green

12 Light green

13 Teal multicolored

14 Light green

Unit C

Unit D

Unit B

¼" seam allowance

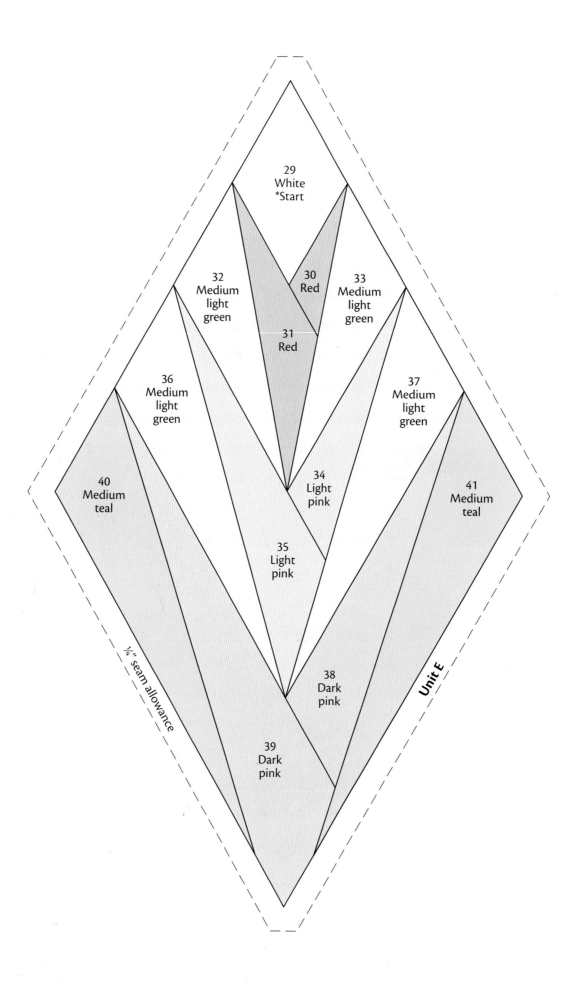

29
White
*Start

32
Medium
light
green

30
Red

33
Medium
light
green

31
Red

36
Medium
light
green

37
Medium
light
green

40
Medium
teal

34
Light
pink

41
Medium
teal

35
Light
pink

¼" seam allowance

38
Dark
pink

Unit E

39
Dark
pink

Thanksgiving Wedding Ring

This quilt features a collection of scraps, including a wide variety of colors, prints, and motifs in different scales, which add eye-catching interest. The fabric choices for the background and border strips are light blue, pink, and gray prints. The medium and dark fabrics used in the foundation-pieced units and in the appliqué include warm prints in reds, golds, and browns, with a few greens tossed into the mix. Even the bias stems are made with a variety of green prints.

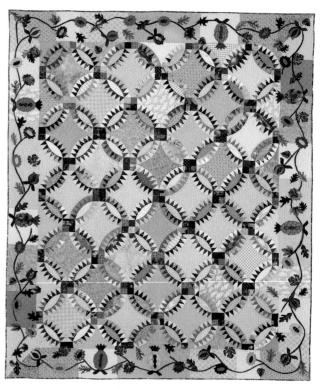

Designed and made by Irene Berry

Finished Quilt: 77½" x 93"
Finished Blocks: 15½"

Materials

- Assorted light print scraps (light blue, pink, and gray), 10 yards *total* for blocks
- Assorted medium and dark print scraps, (reds, golds, browns, and greens), 6 yards *total* for blocks and border appliqués
- Assorted light and medium prints, 2¾ yards *total* for border*
- Assorted green print scraps, ¾ yard *total* for border appliqués
- Gold print, ¾ yard for binding
- Backing, 7½ yards
- Batting, 85" x 101"
- Template plastic

For a border from one fabric, you'll need 2⅞ yards.

Note: Although yardage amounts for foundation piecing are adequate, you may need more if you cut very generous pieces.

Cutting

The appliqué and piecing patterns are on pages 31–33. For detailed instructions, refer to "Making Plastic Templates" on page 91. For accurate piecing, as you cut the A, C, D, and E pieces, mark the placement dots on each, and mark the dots on each arc after it has been foundation pieced.

From the assorted light prints, cut:
  80 pieces with template A
  32 pieces with template C
  14 pieces with template D
  4 pieces with template E

From the assorted medium and dark prints, cut:
  160 squares, 2" x 2" (label as B)
  Appliqué patterns F–P

From the assorted green prints, cut:
  1¼"-wide bias strips, enough to yield 500" total

From the assorted light and medium prints, cut:
  31 border rectangles, 8" x 12"

From the gold print, cut:
  10 binding strips, 2¼" x 42"

Piecing the Units

Refer to "Foundation-Piecing Basics" on page 86 for detailed instructions as needed.

1. Make 160 copies of the arc foundation pattern on page 31.

2. Paper piece the arcs in numerical order in the colors indicated on the pattern. Press and trim after adding each piece.

3. To make a unit, join the arcs to the A and B pieces as shown. It may be helpful to mark and pin at the placement dots. As you sew the curve, stop frequently with the needle in the down position to adjust the fabric. Sew with the foundation-pieced arc on top so you can see the intersecting seam lines and avoid sewing across any of the points. Press the seam allowances toward the A pieces. Make a total of 80 units.

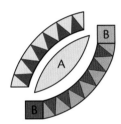 

Make 80.

Making the Quilt Center

1. Arrange the units in a pleasing distribution of colors and prints. Matching the dots, join the units and C pieces to make 20 circular blocks.

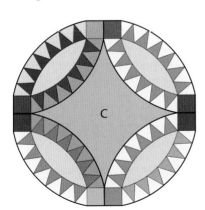

Make 20.

2. Matching dots and points, sew the circular blocks and the remaining C, D, and E pieces together to complete the quilt center as shown in the assembly diagram. When joining the blocks and pieces, remember to sew only on the seam lines and not into the seam allowances. Backstitch at each end to secure the stitching.

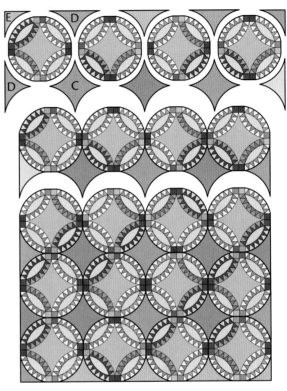

Quilt assembly

Adding the Border

1. For the pieced border, join the 8" x 12" light/medium rectangles end to end to make one long strip. Cut this strip into two 95"-long strips for the side borders and two 80"-long strips for the top and bottom borders.

2. Referring to "Mitered Borders" on page 93, sew the border strips to the quilt and miter the corners. Trim the seam allowances to ¼" and press them open.

3. Remove the paper foundations.

Appliquéing the Border

Irene added her appliqué randomly around the border. For this reason we have not listed the number of pieces required. Have fun choosing and arranging the appliqué pieces to your liking.

1. Following the instructions in "Bias Strips" on page 92, make the bias stems.

2. The appliqué placement and quilting suggestion diagram shows approximate placement of the appliqué and quilting lines. Using this diagram for reference, appliqué the bias stems on the border.

   Notice that the pineapple uses reverse appliqué for the N and O shapes. See "Easy Reverse Appliqué" at right for helpful instructions. Prepare the F–P shapes for "Turned-Edge Appliqué" as described on page 91. In alphabetical order within each motif, appliqué the pieces to the border using a blind stitch.

Appliqué placement and quilting suggestion

Quilting and Finishing

1. Layer and baste together the backing, batting, and quilt top.

2. Refer to the quilting suggestion diagram below left for ideas.

3. Bind the quilt using the 2¼"-wide gold strips.

Easy Reverse Appliqué

To reverse appliqué the N and O shapes, first mark the outline of N on O. With the right side facing up, center the O shape over the N rectangle and baste ¼" outside the marked line. Prepare the outside edges of O for appliqué, and then blindstitch the N/O shape in place on the border. Trim away the O fabric ³⁄₁₆" *inside* the marked line and clip the curves as needed. Turn under the raw edges along the line and blindstitch the folded edge. Remove the basting.

Color Option

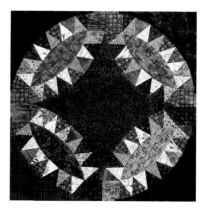

Rings of Gold

For a calming effect, try a color palette of deep reds, blues, greens, and golds. It's helpful to remember that a small amount of yellow, in any shade, goes a long way.

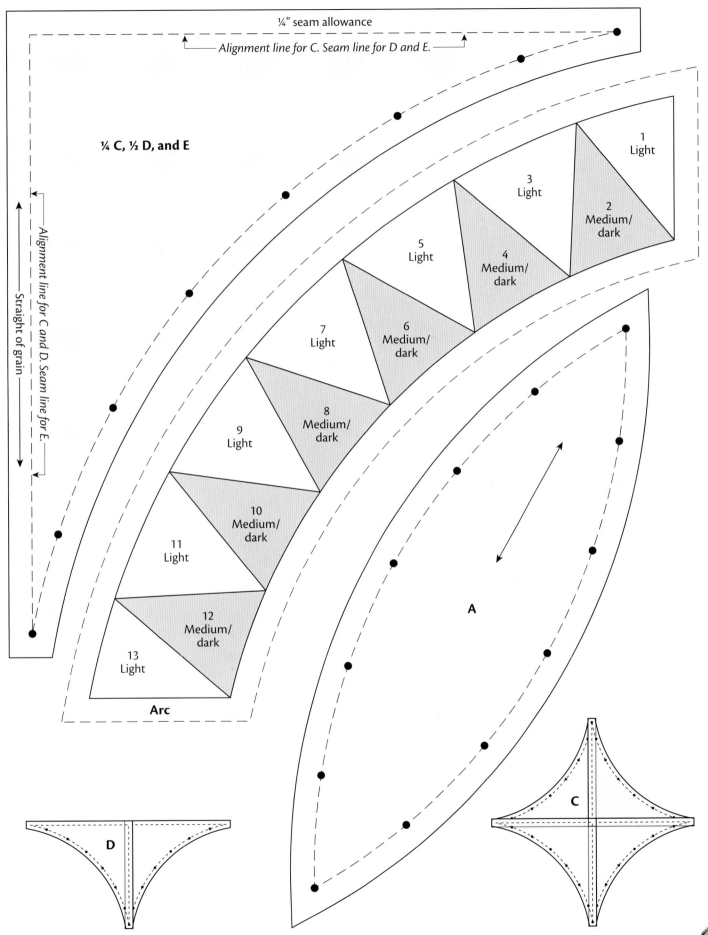

¼" seam allowance

Alignment line for C. Seam line for D and E.

¼ C, ½ D, and E

Alignment line for C and D. Seam line for E.

Straight of grain

1
Light

3
Light

2
Medium/
dark

5
Light

4
Medium/
dark

7
Light

6
Medium/
dark

8
Medium/
dark

9
Light

10
Medium/
dark

11
Light

12
Medium/
dark

13
Light

Arc

A

D

C

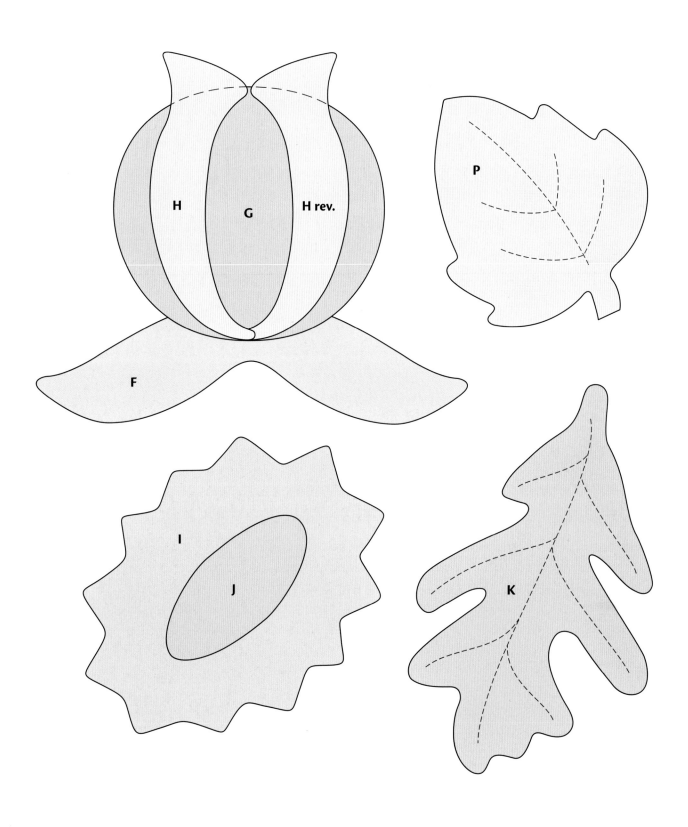

H

G

H rev.

P

F

I

J

K

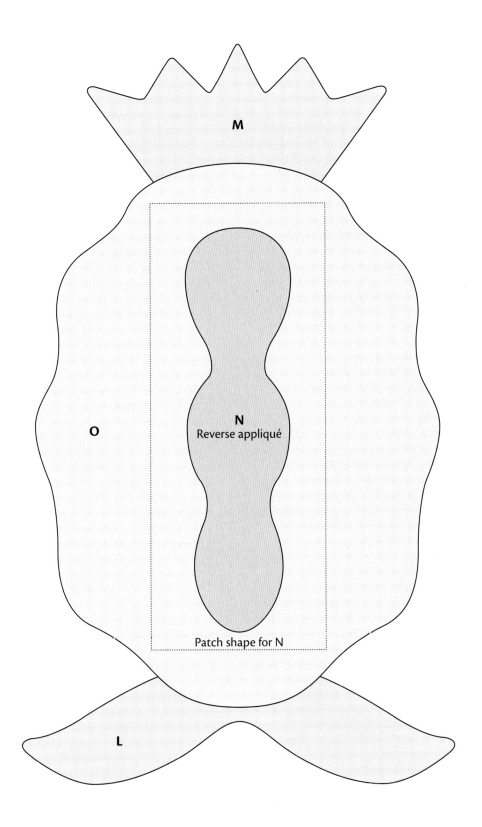

M

O

N
Reverse appliqué

Patch shape for N

L

Goldfish

Finished Quilt: 65½" x 89½"
Finished Blocks: 8½"

Materials

- Gold and orange fabric scraps, 2⅝ yards *total* for blocks
- Blue fabric scraps, 2½ yards *total* for blocks
- Blue-and-orange batik, 2½ yards for outer border
- Blue print, 2⅛ yards for blocks, setting squares and triangles, and pieced border
- Orange print, 1⅞ yards for inner border and binding
- Backing, 5¾ yards
- Batting, 73" x 97"
- Dark brown embroidery floss, 1 skein for fish eyes

Note: Although yardage amounts for foundation piecing are adequate, you may need more if you cut very generous pieces.

Cutting

From the blue print, cut:
    15 squares, 3½" x 3½"
    8 squares, 9" x 9"
    3 squares, 13¼" x 13¼"; cut into quarters
        diagonally to yield 12 triangles
    2 squares, 6⅞" x 6⅞"; cut in half diagonally to
        yield 4 triangles
    42 rectangles, 3¼" x 6¼"
    4 rectangles, 2⅝" x 6"

From the *lengthwise* grain of the orange print, cut:
    2 inner-border strips, 5" x 60½"
    2 inner-border strips, 5" x 45½"
    6 binding strips, 2¼" x 56"

From the *lengthwise* grain of the blue-and-orange batik, cut:
    2 outer-border strips, 5" x 80½"
    2 outer-border strips, 5" x 65½"

Making the Blocks

Refer to "Foundation-Piecing Basics" on page 86 for detailed instructions as needed.

1. Make 102 copies each of the foundation patterns on page 38.

Designed by Marla Stefanelli; made by Mickie Swall

2. Paper piece the units in numerical order in the colors indicated on the pattern. Press and trim after adding each piece.

3. Join the foundation-pieced units to complete the goldfish units. Press the seam allowances toward unit B. Make 102 units.

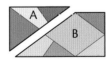

Make 102.

4. Use dark brown thread to satin stitch an eye on each goldfish, stitching through the fabric only. Leave the foundation papers attached for now.

Satin stitch

5. To make block X, sew a goldfish unit to a 3½" blue square, starting from the raw edges and stopping in the center of the square. Working in a counterclockwise direction, join three more fish units to the blue square, and then complete the partial seam. Press the seam allowances toward the blue square. Repeat to make a total of 15 of block X.

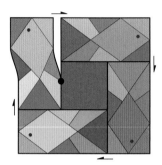

Block X.
Make 15.

Assembling the Quilt Center

1. Referring to the assembly diagram, join the blocks, 9" blue squares, and 13¼" blue triangles in diagonal rows. Press the seam allowances toward the blue squares and triangles.

2. Join the rows and press the seam allowances in one direction. Then sew the 6⅞" blue triangles to the corners and press the seam allowances toward the triangles.

3. Remove the foundation papers from the goldfish units in the X blocks.

Adding Borders

1. Matching centers and ends, sew the 60½"-long orange inner-border strips to the sides of the quilt center. Sew the 45½"-long orange inner-border strips to the top and bottom of the quilt center in the same manner. Press the seam allowances toward the just-added borders.

2. To make the pieced border strips, join 22 gold-fish units to the 3¼" x 6¼" blue rectangles as shown to make the Y blocks.

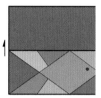

Block Y.
Make 22.

3. Sew the remaining goldfish units to the remaining 3¼" x 6¼" blue rectangles to make the Z blocks.

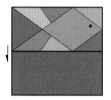

Block Z.
Make 20.

4. Join six Y blocks and six Z blocks to make each pieced side border. For each pieced top and bottom border, join five Y blocks and four Z blocks, and then add a 2⅝" x 6" blue rectangle to each end.

Side border.
Make 2.

Top/bottom border.
Make 2.

5. Matching centers and ends, sew the pieced side border strips to the quilt center, easing as necessary to fit. Press the seam allowances toward the inner border. Add the pieced top and bottom border strips in the same way.

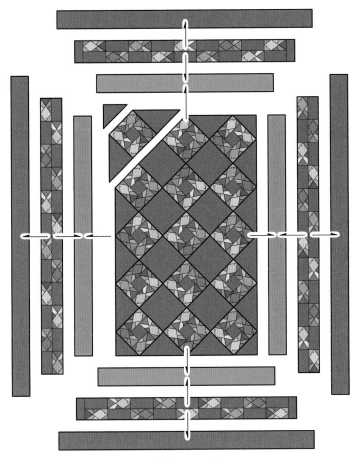

Quilt assembly

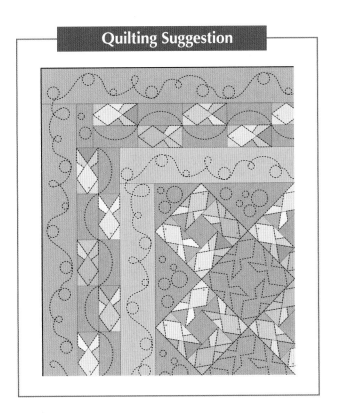

6. Sew the 80½"-long blue-and-orange batik outer-border strips to the sides of the quilt top and press the seam allowances toward the border. Sew the 65½"-long blue-and-orange batik outer-border strips to the top and bottom of the quilt top; press.

7. Remove the foundation papers from the border units.

Quilting and Finishing

1. Layer and baste together the backing, batting, and quilt top.

2. See the quilting suggestion at right.

3. Bind the quilt using the 2¼"-wide orange strips.

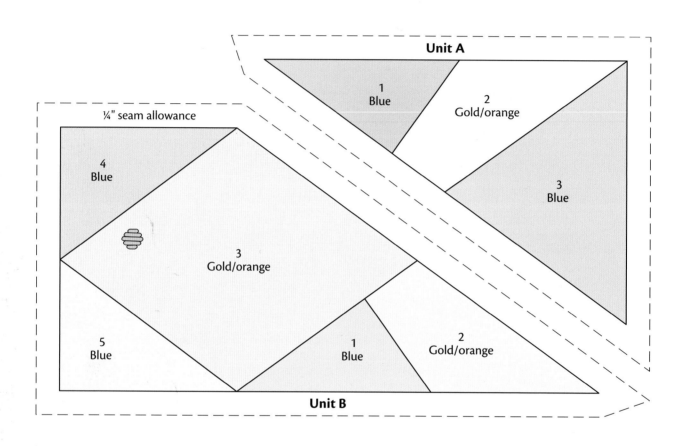

Unit A

1
Blue

2
Gold/orange

3
Blue

¼" seam allowance

4
Blue

3
Gold/orange

5
Blue

1
Blue

2
Gold/orange

Unit B

From My Garden

Designed by Erin Wilcoxon; sewn by Carolyn Beam and
Mickie Swall; quilted by Mickie Swall

Choosing Fabrics

Lots of visually textured fabrics and tone-on-tone prints make these flowers realistic. As you choose your assortment of colors, look for fabrics that range in value from light to dark. You will not need much of any one fabric.

Finished Quilt: 33½" x 31½"
Finished Center: 24" x 22"

Materials

- Dark blue tone-on-tone print, ¾ yard for outer border and binding
- Light cream tone-on-tone print, ⅝ yard for background
- Medium blue tone-on-tone print, ⅓ yard for inner border
- Brown tone-on-tone print, 4" x 15" scrap for bowl
- Brown print, 2" x 15" scrap for bowl rim
- Assorted blue scraps for asters
- Assorted purple scraps for violets
- Assorted red and red-orange scraps for tulips
- Assorted pink scraps for roses and carnations
- Assorted yellow and yellow-orange scraps for roses, asters, and violets
- Assorted green scraps for stems and leaves
- Backing, 1⅜ yards (includes hanging sleeve)
- Batting, 37" x 35"
- White buttons, ½" diameter, 18
- Blue buttons, ½" diameter, 18

Note: Although yardage amounts for foundation piecing are adequate, you may need more if you cut very generous pieces.

Cutting

From the light cream tone-on-tone print, cut:
    1 square, 2½" x 2½"
    1 square, 4½" x 4½"
    2 rectangles, 2½" x 8½"
    1 rectangle, 2½" x 12½"
    2 rectangles, 4½" x 10½"
    1 strip, 2½" x 24½"
    2 squares, 3½" x 3½"
    2 rectangles, 4½" x 5½"

From the brown print, cut:
    1 rectangle, 1½" x 14½"

From the brown tone-on-tone print, cut:
    1 rectangle, 3½" x 14½"

From the assorted green prints, cut:
    4 squares, 2½" x 2½"
    4 A stems
    2 A reversed stems

From the medium blue tone-on-tone print, cut:
    2 inner-border strips, 2" x 24"
    2 inner-border strips, 2" x 29"

From the dark blue tone-on-tone print, cut:
    2 outer-border strips, 3½" x 27"
    2 outer-border strips, 3½" x 35"
    4 binding strips, 2¼" x 42"

Making the Blocks

Refer to "Foundation-Piecing Basics" on page 86 for detailed instructions as needed.

1. Referring to the block diagrams for quantities needed, make the necessary number of each foundation pattern on pages 43–45 to complete the flower blocks.

2. Paper piece the flower and stem blocks and sections in numerical order using the colors indicated in the photo on page 39. Notice that color placement varies between the same flowers. For example, each of the pink roses is slightly different. Press and trim after adding each piece.

3. Join the units as needed to complete each flower, pressing the seam allowances open or away from the bulkier section.

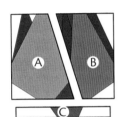

Tulip block.
Make 2.

Stem block.
Make 2.

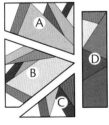 

Carnation block.
Make 2.

Reversed Carnation block.
Make 1.

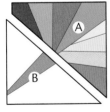 

Aster block.
Make 3.

Rose block.
Make 3.

Violet block.
Make 5.

Assembling the Quilt Top

1. With right sides together, place a 3½" light cream square on a corner of the 3½" x 14½" brown rectangle. Sew from corner to corner as shown. Trim the seam allowances to ¼". Flip the resulting cream triangle open and press the seam allowances toward the brown rectangle. Repeat on the other end of the brown rectangle. Sew the 1½" x 14½" brown rectangle to the top edge to complete the bowl unit.

2. Join the flower and stem blocks, the light cream and green squares, the light cream rectangles, and the bowl unit as shown in the assembly diagram. Remove the paper foundations.

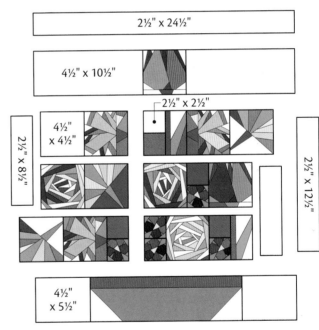

Quilt assembly

3. Prepare the A and A reversed stems as described in "Turned-Edge Appliqué" on page 91. Referring to the quilt photo, casually position the stems on the quilt center. Remove a few stitches in the seams where the stems will be placed. Insert the raw ends of the stems in the seams and restitch the seams. Blindstitch the stems in place.

4. Referring to "Squared Borders" on page 92, measure, cut, and sew the 24"-long medium blue inner-border strips to the sides of the quilt top. Then add the 29"-long medium blue inner-border strips to the top and bottom of the quilt top. Press the seam allowances toward the just-added borders.

5. In the same manner, measure, cut, and sew the 27"-long dark blue outer-border strips to the sides of the quilt top. Then sew the 35"-long dark blue outer-border strips to the top and bottom of the quilt top.

Quilting and Finishing

1. Layer and baste together the backing, batting, and quilt top.

2. In the quilt shown, many of the flowers were machine quilted in the ditch, while pairs of parallel lines were quilted diagonally through the background areas of the quilt. To replicate that look, use ¼"-wide masking tape to mark the angle of the line; then stitch on each side of the tape for parallel lines spaced ¼" apart. The border motifs can be made by tracing the A and A reversed stems and button placement.

3. Sew buttons around the appliquéd stems as shown in the photo on page 39.

4. Bind the quilt using the 2¼"-wide dark blue strips and add a sleeve for hanging.

Quilting Suggestion

Colorwash Garden Option

You can make a simpler version of this quilt by replacing the foundation-pieced flowers with squares of brightly colored floral fabrics, creating a colorwash bouquet.

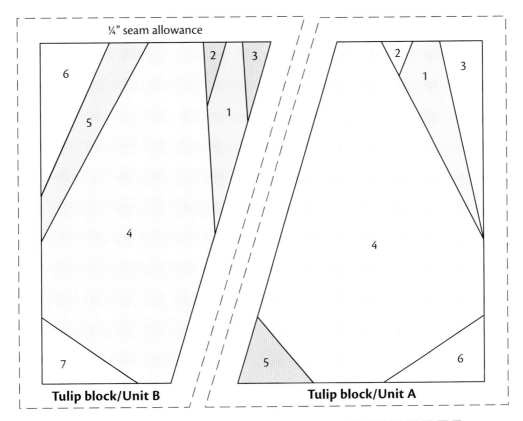

¼" seam allowance

6

5

2 3

1

Tulip block/Unit B

7

2

1

3

4

5 6

Tulip block/Unit A

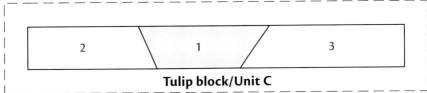

2

1

3

Tulip block/Unit C

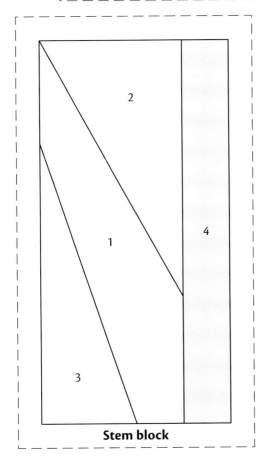

2

1

4

3

Stem block

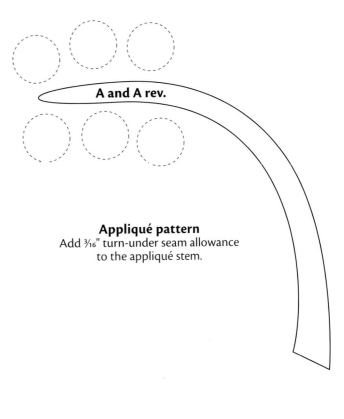

A and A rev.

Appliqué pattern
Add ³⁄₁₆" turn-under seam allowance
to the appliqué stem.

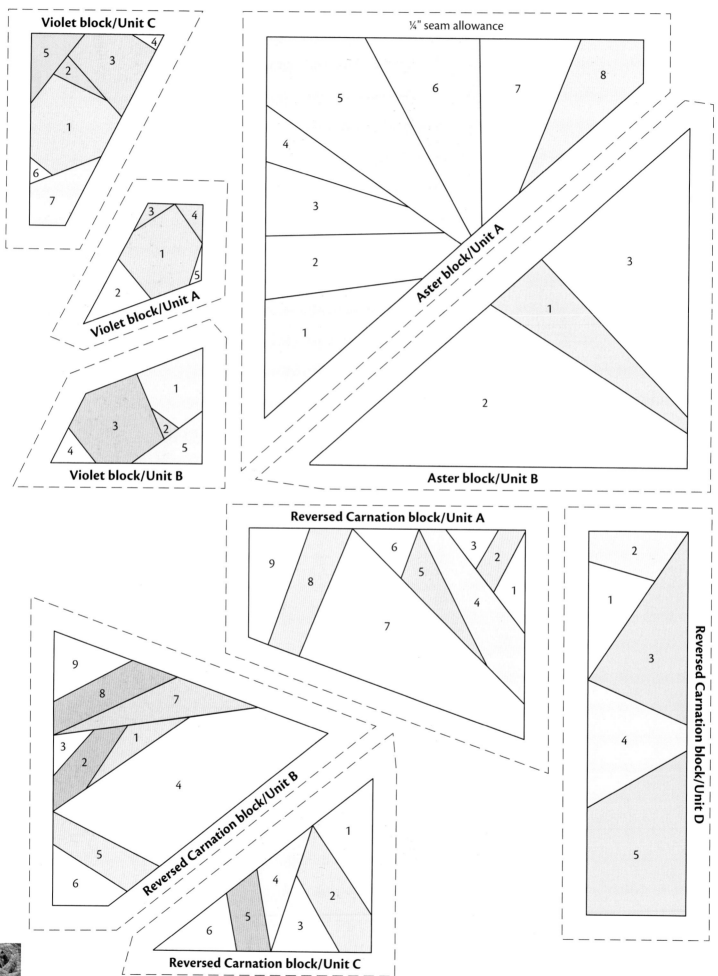

Violet block/Unit C

5 2 3 4

1

6

7

Violet block/Unit A

3 4

1

5

2

Violet block/Unit B

1

3 2

4 5

¼" seam allowance

Aster block/Unit A

5 6 7 8

4

3

2

1

3

1

2

Aster block/Unit B

Reversed Carnation block/Unit A

9 8 6 3 2

5 4 1

7

Reversed Carnation block/Unit D

2

1

3

4

5

Reversed Carnation block/Unit B

9 8 7

3 1

2 4

5

6

Reversed Carnation block/Unit C

1

4 2

5 3

6

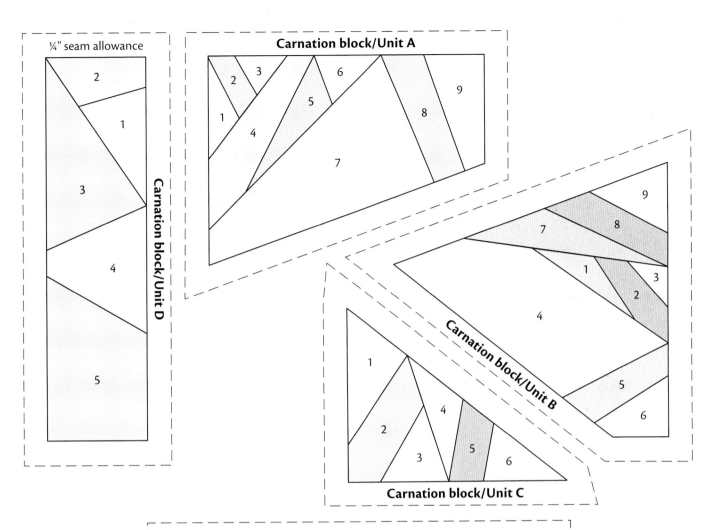

¼" seam allowance

Carnation block/Unit D

2
1
3
4
5

Carnation block/Unit A

2
3
6
1
5
4
8
9
7

9
7
8
1
3
2
4
5
6

Carnation block/Unit B

Carnation block/Unit C

1
2
4
3
5
6

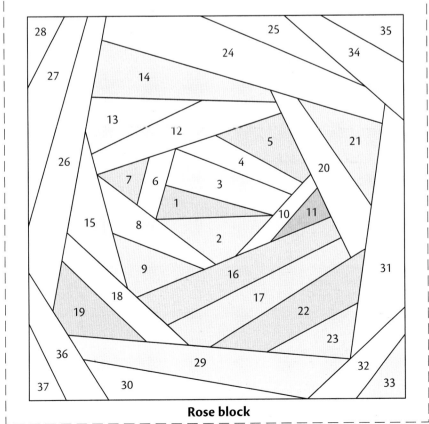

28
27
25
35
24
34
14
13
12
5
21
26
4
7
6
3
20
1
10
11
15
8
2
9
16
31
18
17
19
36
22
23
29
32
37
30
33

Rose block

Great Ball of Fire

Designed and made by Eileen Fowler

Finished Quilt: 50½" x 50½"
Finished Blocks: 6"

Materials

- Dark green batik, 4¼ yards for blocks, inner border, pieced outer border, and binding
- Medium green batik, 1¼ yards for blocks and pieced outer border
- Tan batik, 1¼ yards for blocks and middle border
- Yellow-orange batik, ⅝ yard for blocks
- Orange batik, ⅝ yard for blocks
- Red-orange batik, ⅜ yard for blocks
- Backing, 3⅜ yards
- Batting, 58" x 58"

Note: Although yardage amounts for foundation piecing are adequate, you may need more if you cut very generous pieces.

Cutting

From the medium green batik, cut:
    56 rectangles, 1½" x 3½"
    56 squares, 1½" x 1½"
    56 rectangles, 1½" x 2½"

From the *lengthwise* grain of the dark green batik, cut:
    2 inner-border strips, 2¾" x 36½"
    2 inner-border strips, 2¾" x 41"

From the remaining dark green batik, cut:
    6 binding strips, 2¼" x 42"
    56 rectangles, 1½" x 3½"
    56 squares, 1½" x 1½"
    56 rectangles, 1½" x 2½"
    28 rectangles, 1½" x 6½"
    4 squares, 4½" x 4½"

From the tan batik, cut:
    5 middle-border strips, 1¼" x 42"

Making the Blocks

This quilt uses one off-center Pineapple block with six different colorations. The dark green batik is used in the same positions in all of the blocks. For placement of the other colors, follow the individual block diagrams below. Refer to "Foundation-Piecing Basics" on page 86 for detailed instructions as needed.

1. Make 36 copies of the foundation pattern on page 50.

2. Noting the color placement for each block, paper piece blocks U–Z in numerical order in the colors indicated below. Press and trim after adding each piece. Make the specified number of blocks in each color combination.

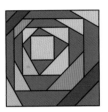

Block U.
Make 4.

Block V.
Make 4.

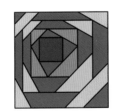

Block W.
Make 8.

Block X.
Make 4.

Block Y.
Make 8.

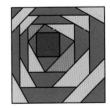

Block Z.
Make 8.

3. Mark a diagonal line on the wrong side of the 1½" medium green and dark green squares, and the 1½" x 2½" medium green rectangles as shown on page 48. Following the diagrams, place a marked square on one end of a 1½" x 3½"

medium green or dark green rectangle, right sides together. Sew on the marked line and trim the seam allowances to ¼". Press the resulting triangle open. In the same manner, sew the marked medium green rectangles to the 1½" x 2½" dark green rectangles. Make 28 of each unit.

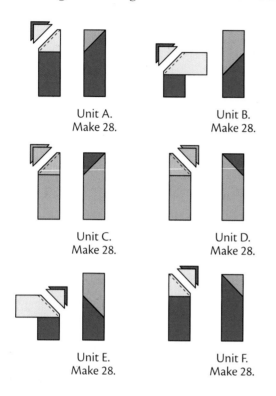

Unit A.
Make 28.

Unit B.
Make 28.

Unit C.
Make 28.

Unit D.
Make 28.

Unit E.
Make 28.

Unit F.
Make 28.

4. Join one each of units A–F as shown. Then sew a 1½" x 6½" dark green rectangle to the top edge to complete a border block. Make 28 blocks.

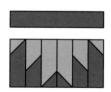
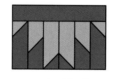

Border block.
Make 28.

Assembling the Quilt Top

1. Noting the block orientations, sew the blocks together in rows as indicated. Press the seam allowances in opposite directions from row to row. Join the rows as shown in the assembly diagram on page 49 and press the seam allowances in one direction.

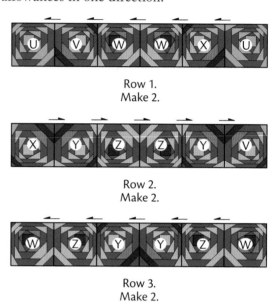

Row 1.
Make 2.

Row 2.
Make 2.

Row 3.
Make 2.

2. Matching centers and ends, sew the 36½"-long dark green inner-border strips to the sides of the quilt top. Sew the 41"-long dark green inner-border strips to the top and bottom of the quilt top in the same way. Press the seam allowances toward the just-added borders.

3. Sew the tan middle-border strips together end to end to make a continuous strip. Referring to "Squared Borders" on page 92, measure, cut, and sew the tan middle-border strips to the sides and then the top and bottom of the quilt top. Press the seam allowances toward the tan border.

4. Join seven border blocks to make a pieced outer-border strip. Make four strips. Sew a 4½" dark green square to each end of the top and bottom strips.

Side border.
Make 2.

Top/bottom border.
Make 2.

5. Matching centers and ends, sew the pieced outer-border strips to the sides and then the top and bottom of the quilt top. Press the seam allowances toward the tan border.

Quilting and Finishing

1. Layer and baste together the backing, batting, and quilt top.

2. See the quilting suggestion below.

3. Bind the quilt using the 2¼"-wide dark green strips.

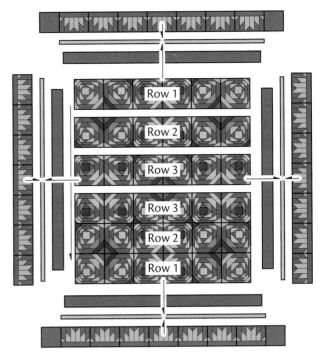

Quilt assembly

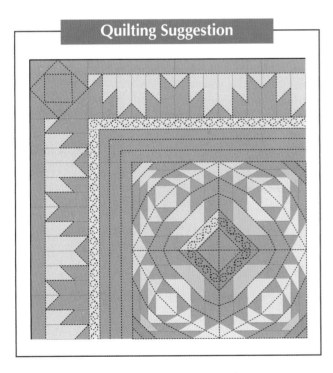

Quilting Suggestion

Color Option

Earth, Wind, and Water

Select a more soothing palette of browns and teals for a table runner with a Southwestern feel. The pattern for "Earth, Wind, and Water" can be found at quiltmaker.com.

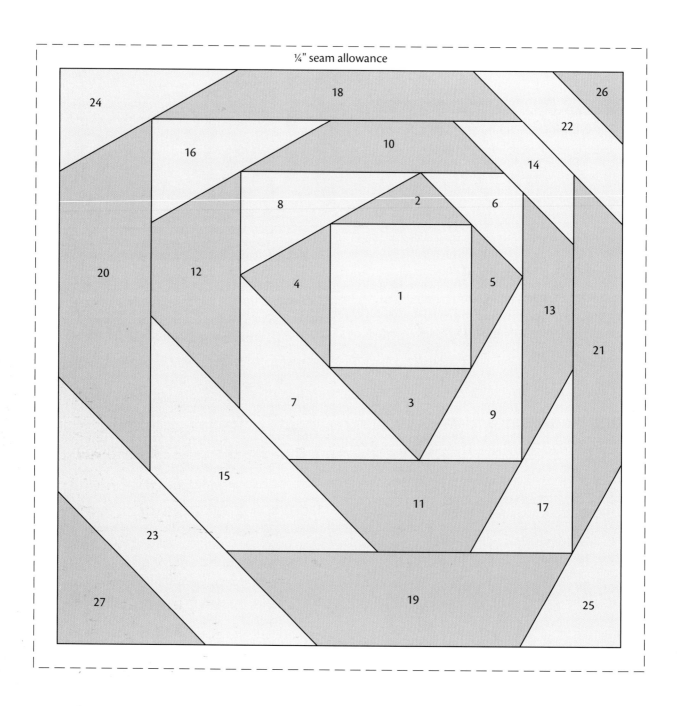

¼" seam allowance

Patriot's Sky

Finished Quilt: 68¾" x 91¼"
Finished Blocks: 11¼"

Materials

- Assorted cream fabrics, 3⅛ yards *total* for blocks
- Assorted red fabrics, 2½ yards *total* for blocks
- Assorted blue fabrics, 1⅔ yards *total* for blocks
- Blue print, 1⅔ yards for inner-border unit
- Beige print, 1⅔ yards for inner-border unit
- Red print, 2½ yards for outer border and binding
- Backing, 5⅞ yards
- Batting, 77" x 99"

Note: Although yardage amounts for foundation piecing are adequate, you may need more if you cut very generous pieces.

Cutting

From the assorted blue fabrics, cut:
    19 squares, 2¾" x 2¾"

From the *lengthwise* grain of the blue print, cut:
    4 strips, 3⅞" x 56¾"
    4 strips, 3⅞" x 34¼"

From the *lengthwise* grain of the beige print, cut:
    2 strips, 5" x 56¾"
    2 strips, 5" x 34¼"

From the *lengthwise* grain of the red print, cut:
    2 outer-border strips, 6½" x 82"
    2 outer-border strips, 6½" x 71"
    5 binding strips, 2¼" x 71"

Making the Blocks

Notice in the photo at right that each block uses one blue for the inner star, one red for the outer star, and assorted cream prints for the background. The red and blue fabrics used in the corners match the fabric in the stars. Refer to "Foundation-Piecing Basics" on page 86 for detailed instructions as needed.

1. Make 76 copies each of the foundation patterns on page 55. Each block requires four of each foundation.

Designed and made by Carolyn McCormick

2. Paper piece the units in numerical order in the colors indicated on the pattern. Press and trim after adding each piece.

3. Sew A and B units together, and then add a C unit. Make four of these sections for each block. Join the four sections, four D units, and a 2¾" blue square to make a block as shown. Make 19 blocks.

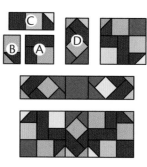

Make 19.

Assembling the Quilt

1. Sew the blocks into five rows of three blocks each as shown. Press the seam allowances in opposite directions from row to row. Sew the rows together and press the seam allowances in one direction.

2. Sew each 56¾"-long beige print strip between two 56¾"-long blue print strips to make two side inner-border units. Press the seam allowances toward the blue strips.

3. Sew each 34¼"-long beige print strip between two 34¼"-long blue print strips to make the top and bottom inner-border strips. Press the seam allowances toward the blue strips. Sew a Star block to both ends of the inner-border strips to complete the top and bottom inner-border units. Press the seam allowances toward the border strips.

4. Matching centers and ends, sew the side inner-border units to the quilt top. Add the top and bottom inner-border units in the same way. Press the seam allowances toward the border units.

5. Referring to "Squared Borders" on page 92, measure, cut, and sew the 82"-long red print outer-border strips to the sides of the quilt top. Then add the 71"-long red print outer-border strips to the top and bottom of the quilt top. Press the seam allowances toward the just-added borders.

6. Remove the foundation papers.

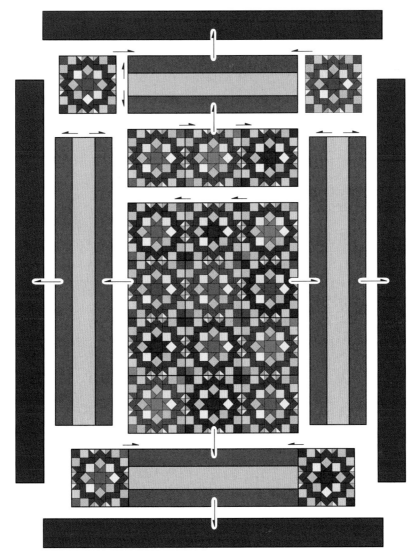

Quilt assembly

Quilting and Finishing

1. Layer and baste together the backing, batting, and quilt top.

2. See the quilting suggestion below. Carolyn's quilt features Baptist fan quilting, which adds lots of visual interest and is appropriate to the original era of this quilt pattern.

3. Bind the quilt using the 2¼"-wide red strips.

Moody Blues

By narrowing the palette to blue and white and using only four different fabrics for the blocks, the overall feeling of this quilt becomes airy and sophisticated.

Quilting Suggestion

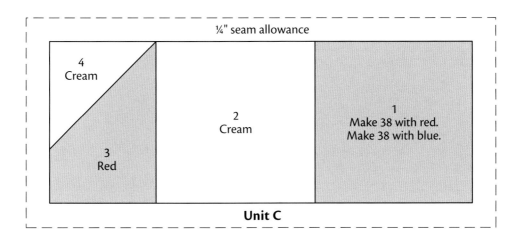

¼" seam allowance

4
Cream

3
Red

2
Cream

1
Make 38 with red.
Make 38 with blue.

Unit C

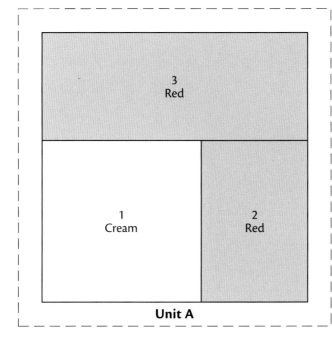

3
Red

1
Cream

2
Red

Unit A

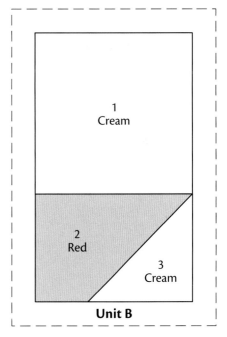

1
Cream

2
Red

3
Cream

Unit B

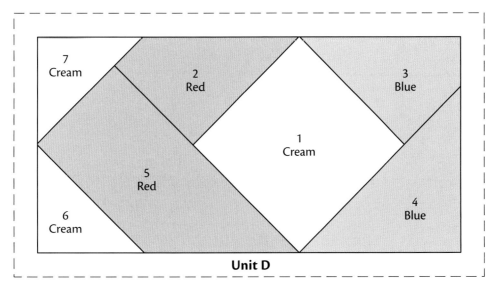

7
Cream

2
Red

3
Blue

1
Cream

5
Red

4
Blue

6
Cream

Unit D

Bow-dacious

Finished Quilt: 72½" x 100½"
Finished Blocks: 6" x 9"

Materials

- Soft yellow print, 7¾ yards for blocks, borders, and binding
- Assorted medium prints, 17 assorted 7" x 10" pieces for center bows
- Assorted light prints, 17 assorted 8" x 10" pieces for center bows
- Assorted dark tone-on-tone fabrics, 17 assorted scraps (at least 1½" x 3") for center bow knots
- Medium blue print, 1⅛ yards for border bows
- Light blue print, 1⅞ yards for borders and border bows
- Dark blue tone-on-tone fabrics, ⅛ yard for border bow knots
- Backing, 6½ yards
- Batting, 80" x 108"

Note: Although yardage amounts for foundation piecing are adequate, you may need more if you cut very generous pieces.

Cutting

From the *lengthwise* grain of the soft yellow print, cut:
 2 outer-border strips, 3½" x 97"
 2 outer-border strips, 3½" x 75"
 2 inner-border strips, 6½" x 63½"
 2 inner-border strips, 7" x 48½"*
 8 binding strips, 2¼" x 48"
 10 squares, 9½" x 9½"

From the remaining soft yellow print, cut:
 5 strips, 6½" x 42"
 8 rectangles, 8" x 9½"

From the light blue print, cut:
 5 strips, 3½" x 42"
 4 rectangles, 3½" x 9½"

*The top/bottom inner-border strips are intentionally ½" wider than the side-border strips.

Quilt designed by Theresa Eisinger; Bow pattern designed by Carol Vyncke; quilt was made by Peg Spradlin

Making the Bow Blocks

Each Bow block uses a light print and a medium print in the same hue. Scraps of a darker tone-on-tone fabric give the center "knot" dimension. Notice that two of the bows in the quilt center are made from the blue fabrics used in the bow border. Refer to "Foundation-Piecing Basics" on page 86 for detailed instructions as needed.

1. Make 37 copies each of the bow foundation patterns on page 61.

2. Paper piece the units in numerical order as indicated on the pattern. Each Bow block uses one light print and one medium print of the same color and one dark tone-on-tone scrap for two of the knot pieces. Press and trim after

adding each piece. Make a total of 17 Bow blocks in a variety of colors.

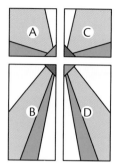 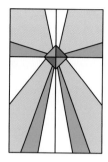

Bow block.
Make 17 with
assorted prints.

3. In the same way, make 20 Bow blocks from the light blue print and the medium blue print, adding dark blue tone-on-tone scraps to the knot. Set the blue Bow blocks aside for the border.

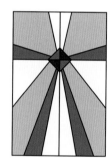

Border bow.
Make 20 with
blue prints.

Assembling the Quilt Top

1. Arrange the assorted Bow blocks on a design wall to find a pleasing arrangement.

2. For row 1, sew a 9½" soft yellow square between two Bow blocks. Add an 8" x 9½" soft yellow rectangle to each end to complete the row. Press the seam allowances toward the soft yellow pieces. Make four of row 1.

3. For row 2, sew three Bow blocks and two 9½" soft yellow squares together as shown in the assembly diagram on page 60. Press the seam allowances toward the soft yellow squares. Make three of row 2.

4. Sew the rows together to complete the quilt center. Press the seam allowances in one direction.

5. Sew a 3½" x 42" light blue print strip and a 6½" x 42" soft yellow strip together along one long edge to make a strip set. Make five strip sets. Cut four strip sets into 16 segments, 8½" wide. Cut the remaining strip set into four segments, 6½" wide.

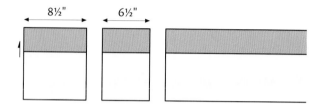

6. For each side border strip, sew six border Bow blocks and five 8½"-wide segments together as shown. Press the seam allowances toward the segments. Make two border strips. For the top border strip, sew four border Bow blocks and three 8½"-wide segments together, starting with a Bow block. Add a 6½"-wide segment and a light blue rectangle to each end of the strip as shown to complete the border strip. Repeat to make the bottom border strip.

Side border.
Make 2.

Top/bottom border.
Make 2.

7. Matching centers and ends, sew the 63½"-long soft yellow inner-border strips to the sides of the quilt center. Sew the 48½"-long soft yellow top and bottom strips to the quilt top. Again matching centers and ends, sew the bow border strips to the sides and then the top and bottom of the quilt top. Pay attention to the orientation of the blue bows across the top of the quilt. Press the seam allowances as indicated in the assembly diagram.

For perfect placement of odd-angle pieces, place the printed side of the foundation face up and identify the area you need to cover; in this case it's piece 2 (the fabric for piece 1 is already positioned). Place the fabric for piece 2 right side down on top of area 2, making sure the grain line is parallel to the sides of the block and that the fabric extends more than ¼" beyond the seam line on all sides of area 2.

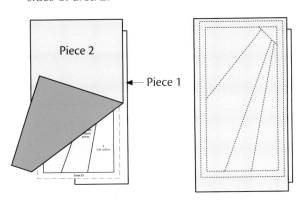

Fold the fabric along the printed line toward the area you're covering and finger-press. This will be your seam line. Trim away the top layer, estimating a ¼" seam allowance. Discard the trimmed fabric; the bottom layer will be stitched to the foundation.

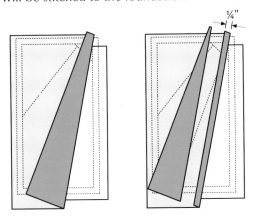

Using an easily visible marking tool, mark each end of the printed seam line on the newly trimmed seam allowance.

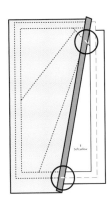

Place piece 2 on the unprinted side of the foundation, right sides together with piece 1, and align the marks with the ends of the printed seam line. The trimmed seam allowance on piece 2 should extend into area 2. Holding the pieces in place, sew on the printed seam line. Trim the seam allowances for pieces 1 and 2 to make a ¼" seam allowance as needed.

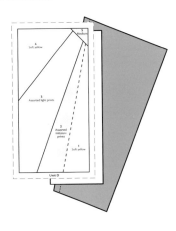

8. Referring to "Squared Borders" on page 92, measure, cut, and sew the 97"-long soft yellow outer-border strips to the sides of the quilt top. Then add the 75"-long soft yellow outer-border strips to the top and bottom of the quilt top. Press the seam allowances toward the just-added borders.

9. Remove the foundation papers.

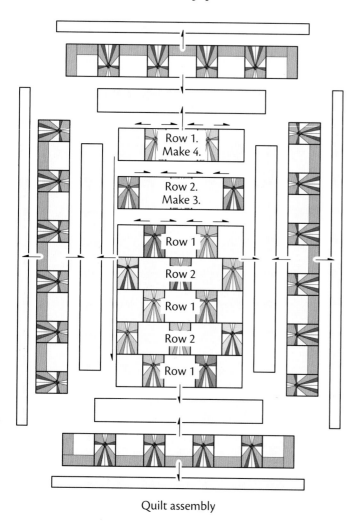

Row 1.
Make 4.

Row 2.
Make 3.

Row 1

Row 2

Row 1

Row 2

Row 1

Quilt assembly

Quilting and Finishing

1. Layer and baste together the backing, batting, and quilt top.

2. See the quilting suggestion upper right. The quilt shown has feathered hearts quilted in the open areas in the quilt center, and a crosshatching pattern in the bow borders.

3. Bind the quilt using the 2¼"-wide soft yellow strips.

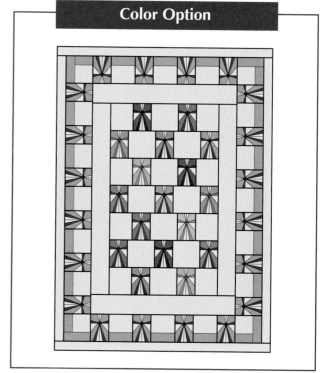

Color Option

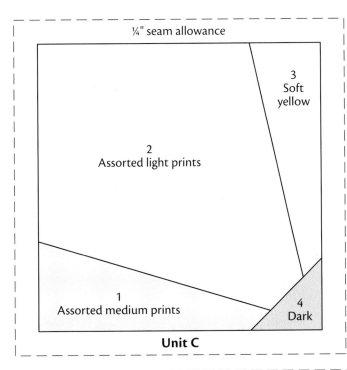

¼" seam allowance

3
Soft yellow

2
Assorted light prints

1
Assorted medium prints

4
Dark

Unit C

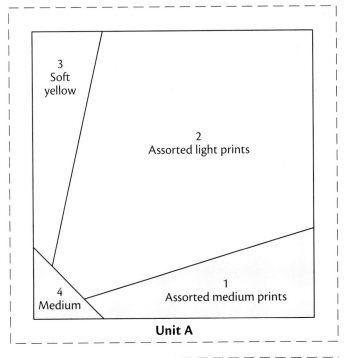

3
Soft yellow

2
Assorted light prints

4
Medium

1
Assorted medium prints

Unit A

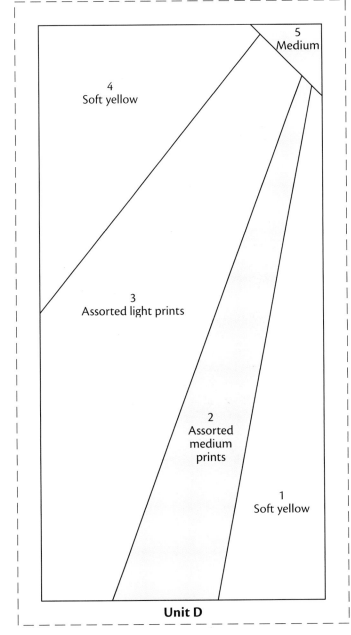

5
Medium

4
Soft yellow

3
Assorted light prints

2
Assorted medium prints

1
Soft yellow

Unit D

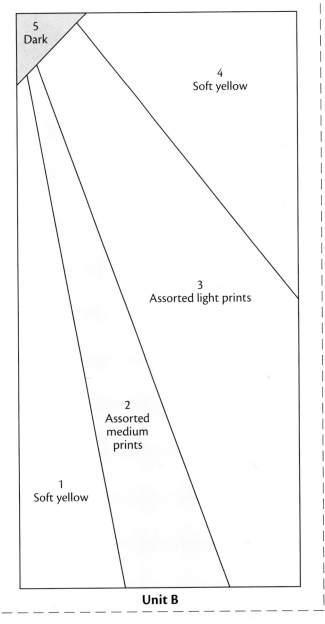

5
Dark

4
Soft yellow

3
Assorted light prints

2
Assorted medium prints

1
Soft yellow

Unit B

Noah's Arks

Finished Quilt: 67½" x 89½"
Finished Blocks: 9" x 7"

Materials

- Light blue print, 4 yards for block backgrounds/ sky
- Dark blue print, 2⅝ yards for sashing strips, side inner borders, and outer border
- Assorted blue scraps, 2 yards *total* for water
- Assorted bright prints, 40 scraps, at least 3" x 8", for arks
- Assorted bright prints, 40 scraps, at least 2" x 8", for roofs
- Assorted animal prints, 40 scraps, at least 2" x 3½", for 40 animals*
- Turquoise striped fabric, ¾ yard for binding
- Backing, 4½ yards
- Batting, 75" x 97"
- Template plastic

See "How Much Is That Zebra in the Window?" for more information on cutting the animal-print rectangles.

Note: Although yardage amounts for foundation piecing are adequate, you may need more if you cut very generous pieces.

Cutting

From the *lengthwise* grain of the dark blue print, cut:
    2 inner-border strips, 5" x 67½"
    2 outer-border strips, 4½" x 84"
    2 outer-border strips, 4½" x 70"
    8 sashing strips, 2¾" x 36½"

From the turquoise striped fabric, cut:
    9 strips, 2¼" x 42"

Making the Blocks

Refer to "Foundation-Piecing Basics" on page 86 for detailed instructions as needed.

1. Make 28 copies each of the ark 1 and ark 2 foundation patterns on pages 66 and 67. Note that 20 of each foundation will be used to piece the arks. The remaining foundations will be used to piece the Sea 1 and Sea 2 blocks.

Designed by Brenda Groelz; made by Mickie Swall

How Much Is That Zebra in the Window?

The window piece is fairly small, so you'll want to place animals in the windows carefully. Draw a 1¼" x 3" rectangle on transparent template plastic. Add a ¼" seam allowance all around, and then cut out the window template on the outer lines. Place the template on your fabric, capturing the animal in exactly the position you want. Trace around the template, cut out your animal, and position it for piece 1 on the foundation.

2. Paper piece the Ark blocks in numerical order using the colors indicated in the diagrams below and in the photo on page 63. Press and trim after adding each piece. See the tip "How Much Is That Zebra in the Window?" on page 63 for exact placement of the animals in piece 1. Make 20 of each block.

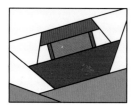
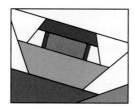

Ark 1.
Make 20.

Ark 2.
Make 20.

3. To make the Sea 1 and Sea 2 blocks, cut 16 light blue (sky) pieces, 7" x 10". Cover pieces 1–12 on each ark 1 or ark 2 foundation with a sky piece; then add blue (water) fabric for pieces 13 and 14. Make eight of each block.

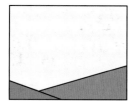
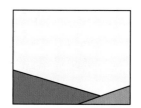

Sea 1.
Make 8.

Sea 2.
Make 8.

Assembling the Quilt

1. Sew the blocks together into rows as shown. Press the seam allowances in one direction.

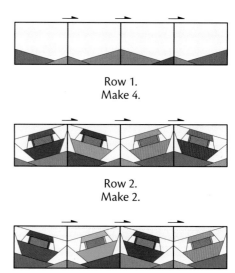

Row 1.
Make 4.

Row 2.
Make 2.

Row 3.
Make 1.

2. Referring to the assembly diagram, sew a 36½"-long dark blue sashing strip to the bottom of each block row, matching centers and ends and easing to fit if necessary. In the same way, join the rows and add a dark blue sashing strip to the top row to complete the quilt center.

3. Matching centers and ends, sew the 67½"-long dark blue inner-border strips to the sides of the quilt. Press the seam allowances toward the inner border.

4. For the pieced border, join five Ark blocks as shown in the assembly diagram to make the top border strip. Repeat to make the bottom border strip. Sew the border strips to the quilt, matching centers and ends and orienting them as shown. Press the seam allowances toward the quilt center.

5. Join nine Ark blocks to make each side border strip, and then sew them to the quilt sides, matching centers and ends and pressing as before.

6. Referring to "Squared Borders" on page 92, measure, cut, and sew the 84"-long dark blue outer-border strips to the sides of the quilt top. Then add the 70"-long dark blue outer-border strips to the top and bottom of the quilt top. Press the seam allowances toward the just-added borders.

7. Remove the foundation papers.

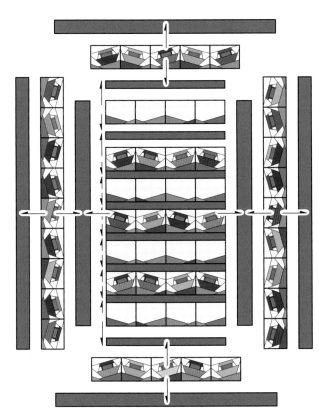

Quilt assembly

Quilting and Finishing

1. Layer and baste together the backing, batting, and quilt top.

2. See the quilting suggestion below.

3. Bind the quilt using the 2¼"-wide turquoise striped strips.

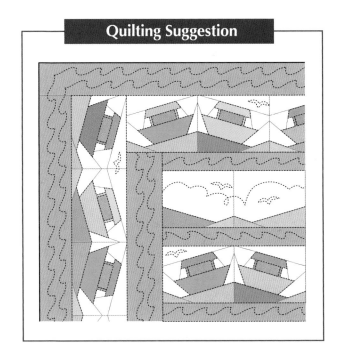

Quilting Suggestion

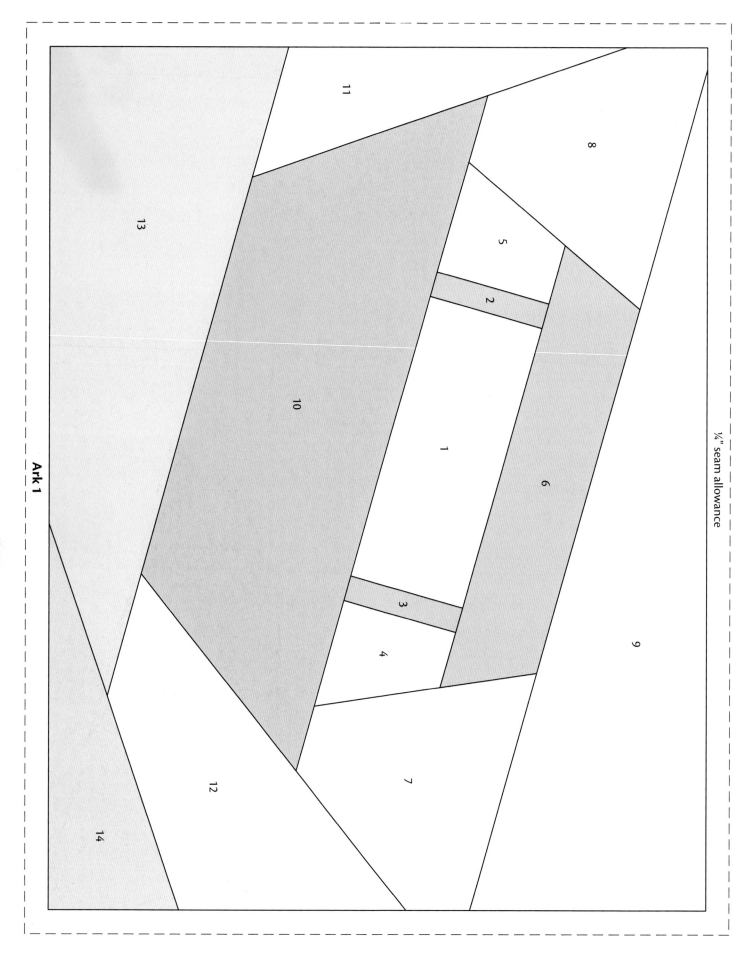

Ark 1

¼" seam allowance

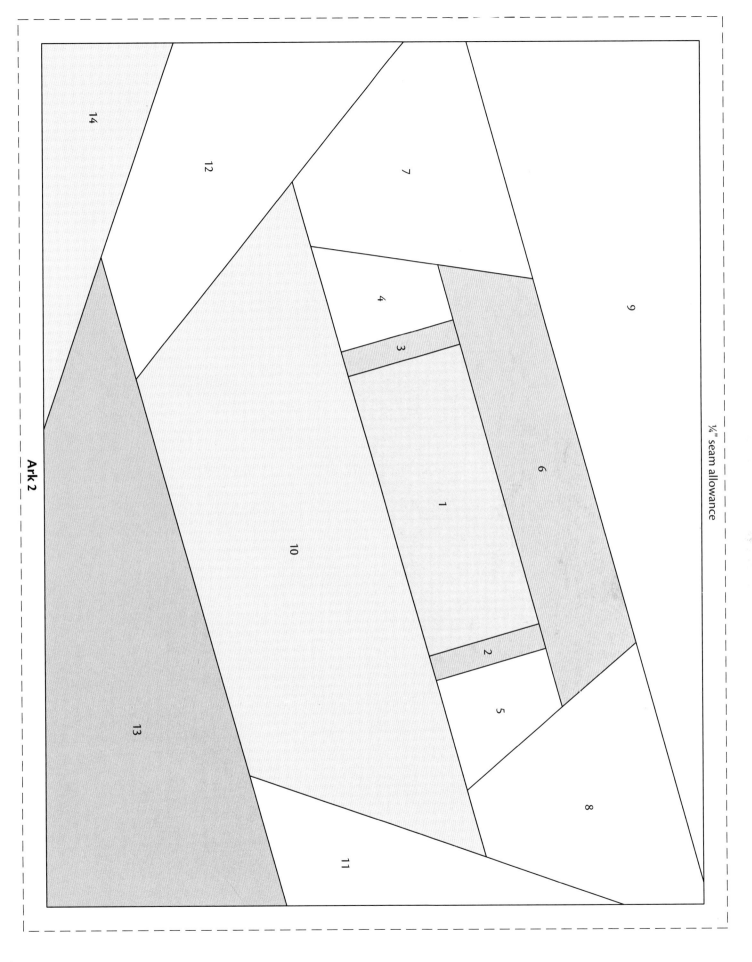

Ark 2

¼" seam allowance

Forever Green

Finished Tree Skirt: 44" x 44"
Finished Blocks: 7½"

Materials

- Dark green fabric*, 1 yard for trees
- Red tone-on-tone fabric, ⅞ yard for binding and prairie-point edging
- Pale green fabric, ⅝ yard for center square and setting triangles
- White print*, ⅝ yard for tree backgrounds
- Medium green fabric, ⅓ yard for block frames
- Red floral, ⅓ yard for center triangles
- Medium pink fabric, ⅛ yard for block corners
- Brown fabric*, ⅛ yard for tree trunks
- Backing, 3 yards
- Batting, 49" x 49"

Although fabric amounts are adequate for foundation piecing, you may need more if you cut very generous pieces.

Cutting

From the medium green fabric, cut:
    20 rectangles, 2" x 8"

From the pale green fabric, cut:
    1 square, 8" x 8"
    4 squares, 8⅜" x 8⅜"; cut in half diagonally to
        yield 8 triangles

From the red floral, cut:
    2 squares, 8⅜" x 8⅜"; cut in half diagonally to
        yield 4 triangles

From the red tone-on-tone fabric, cut:
    5 bias strips, 2½" x 17"
    64 squares, 3" x 3"

From the medium pink fabric, cut:
    20 squares, 2" x 2"

Making the Blocks

Refer to "Foundation-Piecing Basics" on page 86 for detailed instructions as needed.

1. Make eight copies each of the tree foundation patterns for units A and B on page 73. *Please notice that the foundation has been printed without*

Tree skirt designed by Theresa Eisinger;
Tree block designed by Pat Madorin; made by Mickie Swall

seam allowances. Allow a generous ¼" of fabric beyond the perimeter of the unit when sewing.

2. Paper piece the units in numerical order in the colors indicated on the pattern. Press and trim after adding each piece. Complete each unit by trimming the excess fabric, leaving ¼" beyond the edge of the paper. One way to do this is to align the paper's edge with the ¼" line on a rotary-cutting ruler and trim away the excess fabric.

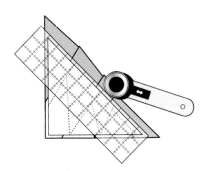

3. Repeat to make eight of tree unit A and eight of tree unit B.

4. Join an A unit to each B unit to make a total of eight Tree blocks. Press the seam allowances open.

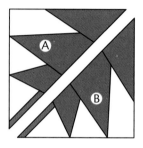 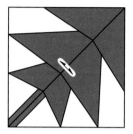

Make 8.

5. Sew medium green rectangles to opposite sides of a Tree block. Then sew a medium pink square to each end of two of the medium green rectangles. Sew these to the top and bottom of the tree to complete a framed Tree block. Press all seam allowances toward the medium green rectangles. Repeat to make a total of four blocks.

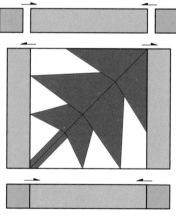

Make 4.

6. To make the plain framed block for the center of the tree skirt, sew the remaining medium green rectangles, pink squares, and 8" pale green square together as shown. Sew a red floral triangle to each side of the center block. Press the seam allowances open.

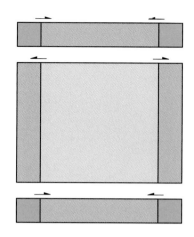

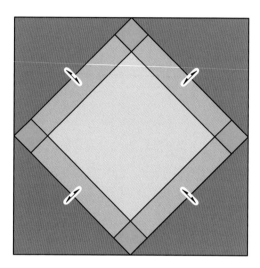

Assembling the Tree Skirt

1. Sew pale green triangles to the two upper sides of each framed Tree block as shown. Press the seam allowances open.

2. Referring to the assembly diagram, lay out the plain Tree blocks, framed tree sections, and center block in rows as shown. Join the pieces into rows, and then sew the rows together. Press the seam allowances toward the pale green triangles.

Tree-skirt assembly

Marking and Partial Quilting

1. Using the patchwork as a guide, mark a 1½" grid in the center of the tree skirt as shown in the quilting suggestion diagram. Mark free-form boughs in the Tree blocks, or plan to quilt the trees without marking.

2. Layer the backing, batting, and tree-skirt top; baste the layers together. Quilt the grid and the free-form boughs. *Do not* quilt the outer edges of the tree skirt and the tree trunks until *after* the prairie points have been added to the edges.

Quilting suggestion

3. Trim the backing and batting even with the tree-skirt top.

Adding the Prairie Points

1. To make the prairie points, fold the 3" red squares in half diagonally, wrong sides together; then fold diagonally again and press.

2. Pin the tree-skirt backing away from the edges. On the top of the tree skirt, align five prairie points along each of the framed Tree block edges and three prairie points along each edge of the remaining Tree blocks, overlapping the prairie points slightly; there will be about 2" between the tips of the points. The points should face toward the center of the tree skirt as shown.

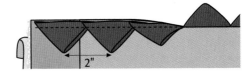

3. Using a walking foot on your machine, sew ¼" from the raw edges through the prairie points, tree-skirt top, and batting. Trim the excess bulk in the seam allowances at the corners. Press the seam allowances toward the center to make the prairie points face outward. Unpin the backing, fold it under ¼", and pin in place; then blindstitch in place.

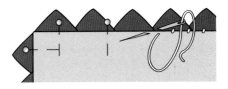

4. Outline quilt the edge of the tree skirt and around the tree trunks.

Making the Center Opening and Finishing

1. The center opening will need to be about 5" in diameter. You can make a circular template and trace around it, or find a round object with a diameter of about 5" to place in the center of the center block and trace. (Note: A computer CD is about 4¾" in diameter, so you could use an old one of those, but then you'll need to draw another line about ¼" outside of the traced line.)

2. Beginning at the bottom of a plain Tree block (one without a frame), cut a straight line up the center of the block to the marked circle. Cut out the circle.

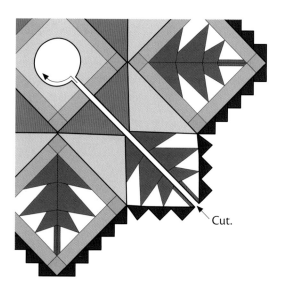

Cut.

3. Join enough bias strips to make a 66"-long strip. Starting at the bottom of the tree trunk and leaving a ½" tail, sew the binding to the tree-skirt opening, mitering at the circle corners.

Smooth Binding around the Circle

As you sew the inner circle, slightly stretch the binding strip around the edge. This will help to eliminate puckers when the binding is wrapped to the back of the quilt.

4. Cut off the strip ½" from the tree-skirt edge. Fold the binding ends under ½" and blindstitch the binding to the back of the tree skirt as shown.

Color Option

I'll Have a Blue Christmas

If traditional holiday colors don't complement your decor, try something in blue! The background print, reminiscent of a 1960s Christmas card, was the starting point of this color scheme. If you choose to use stripes or directional prints like those shown here, you will want to pay special attention to their orientation, which means you may need additional yardage.

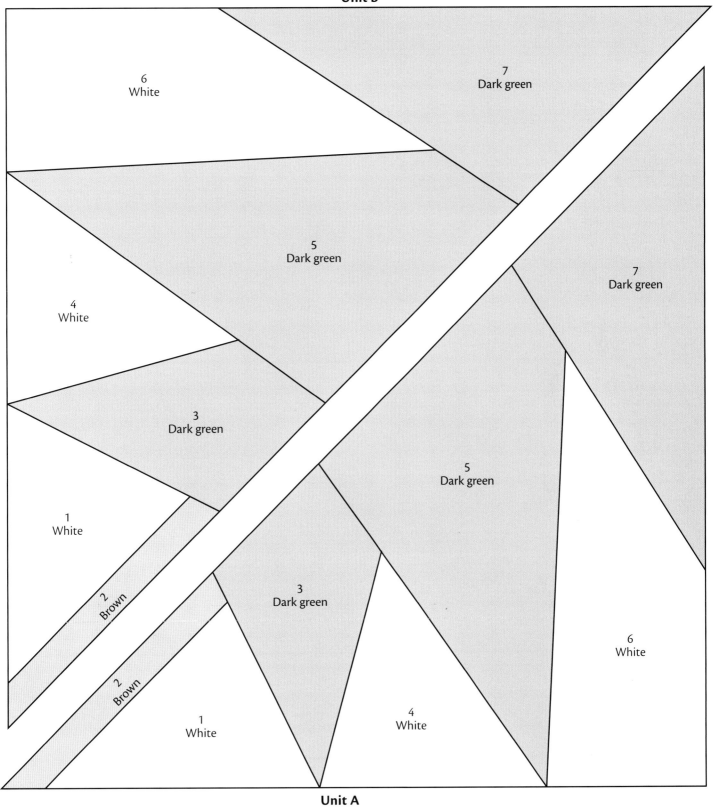

6
White

7
Dark green

5
Dark green

7
Dark green

4
White

3
Dark green

1
White

5
Dark green

2
Brown

2
Brown

3
Dark green

6
White

1
White

4
White

Unit A

Hanukkah Lights

Finished Wall Hanging: 35" x 22½"
Finished Table Runner: 22½" x 40"

Materials for Wall Hanging

- Dark purple print, ½ yard for blocks and background
- Green-and-purple print, ½ yard for inner border and binding
- Dark blue tone-on-tone fabric, ½ yard for outer border
- Assorted gold prints, ¼ yard *total* for candlesticks
- Yellow tone-on-tone fabric, 2" x 14" piece for flames
- Assorted light blue prints, scraps for candles (9 pieces, at least 1½" x 2" each)
- Backing and sleeve, 1⅛ yards
- Batting, 27" x 39"

Note: Although yardage amounts for foundation piecing are adequate, you may need more if you cut very generous pieces.

Cutting for Wall Hanging

From the dark purple print, cut:
  2 rectangles, 1¾" x 10½"
  1 strip, 1¾" x 23"

From the assorted gold prints, cut:
  1 strip, 1¾" x 23"
  Use remaining gold prints for candlesticks.

From the green-and-purple print, cut:
  2 inner-border strips, 2" x 13"
  2 inner-border strips, 2" x 28"
  4 binding strips, 2¼" x 42"

From the dark blue tone-on-tone fabric, cut:
  2 outer-border strips, 5" x 16"
  2 outer-border strips, 5" x 36"

From the backing fabric, cut:
  1 panel, 27" x 39"
  1 strip, 9" x 34"

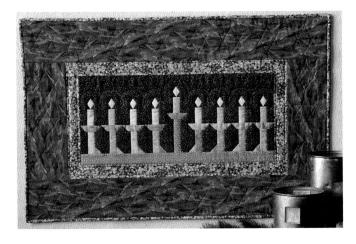

Based on the "Festival of Lights" pattern designed by Helen Bachtell; made by Cindy Erickson

Making the Menorah Block

Refer to "Foundation-Piecing Basics" on page 86 for detailed instructions as needed.

1. Using the foundation patterns on page 79, make four copies each of unit A and unit B, one copy of unit C, and nine copies of unit D.

2. Paper piece the units in numerical order in the colors indicated on the pattern, using the dark purple print for all of the background pieces. Press and trim after adding each piece.

3. Sew the sections together as shown to make the number of candles indicated.

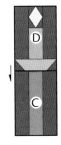

Unit A/D.
Make 4.

Unit B/D.
Make 4.

Unit C/D.
Make 1.

4. Join the four A/D units, and then add a 1¾" x 10½" dark purple rectangle to the top edge. In the same way, join the four B/D units and add a dark purple rectangle on top. Sew these sections to either side of the tall candlestick (unit C/D) to complete the Menorah block.

5. Add the gold strip to the bottom of the Menorah block and the 23"-long dark purple strip to the top. Press the seam allowances toward the strips. Remove the paper foundations.

Make 1 for wall hanging.
Make 2 for table runner.

Adding the Borders

1. Referring to "Squared Borders" on page 92, measure, cut, and sew the 13"-long green-and-purple inner-border strips to the sides of the quilt. Add the 28"-long green-and-purple inner-border strips to the top and bottom of the quilt in the same way. Press the seam allowances toward the just-added strips.

2. Repeat to add the dark blue outer-border strips.

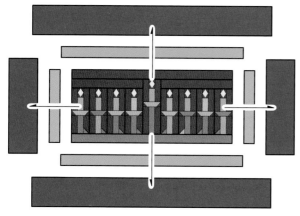

Wall-hanging assembly

Quilting and Finishing

If desired, mark any quilting patterns on the quilt top before layering and basting.

1. Layer and baste together the backing, batting, and quilt top.

2. See the quilting suggestion below.

3. Bind the quilt using the 2¼"-wide green-and-purple strips.

4. Use the 9"-wide strip of backing fabric to add a sleeve for hanging.

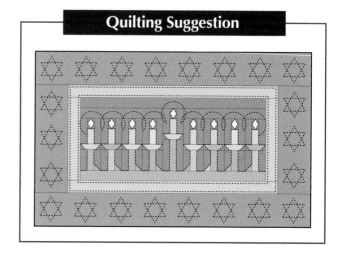

Quilting Suggestion

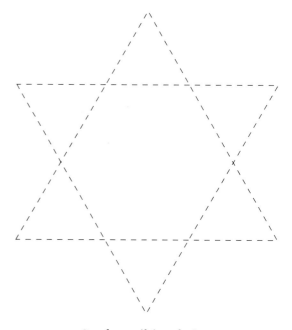

Border quilting design

Hanukkah Lights Table Runner

Materials for Table Runner

- Dark purple print, 1½ yards for blocks, background, and binding
- Assorted gold prints, ⅜ yard *total* for candlesticks
- Yellow tone-on-tone fabric, 2" x 14" piece for flames
- Assorted light blue prints, scraps for candles (18 pieces, at least 1½" x 2" each)
- Backing, 1⅜ yards
- Batting, 27" x 44"

Cutting for Table Runner

From the dark purple print, cut:
    1 square, 23" x 23"
    4 strips, 1¾" x 10½"
    4 binding strips, 2¼" x 42"

From the assorted gold prints, cut:
    2 strips, 1¾" x 23"
    Use remaining gold prints for candlesticks.

If you'd like a longer table runner, you can cut a rectangle instead of a square for the center section. With a square center, the table runner will finish at 40" long. Determine the length you'd like your table runner to be and add the difference to the cut size. For example, if you'd like a 54"-long table runner, 54" – 40" = 14". Add the 14" difference to the dimension of the cut piece, or cut a 23" x 37" rectangle.

Remember, you'll need to adjust the batting and backing sizes accordingly.

Making the Table Runner

Refer to "Foundation-Piecing Basics" on page 86 for detailed instructions as needed.

1. Using the foundation patterns on page 79, make eight copies each of unit A and unit B, two copies of unit C, and 18 copies of unit D.

2. Make two Menorah blocks as described in steps 2 through 4 of "Making the Menorah Block" on page 75.

3. Sew a gold strip to the bottom of each block and press the seam allowances toward the strip.

4. Sew the blocks to opposite sides of the dark purple square as shown in the assembly diagram. Press the seam allowances toward the dark purple square.

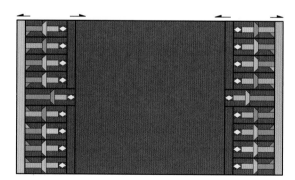

Table-runner assembly

Quilting and Finishing

1. Layer and baste together the backing, batting, and quilt top.

2. See the quilting suggestion below.

3. Bind the quilt using the 2¼"-wide dark purple strips.

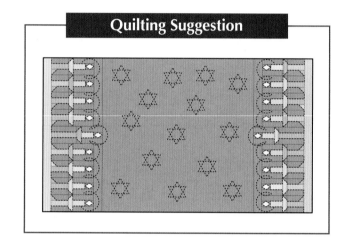

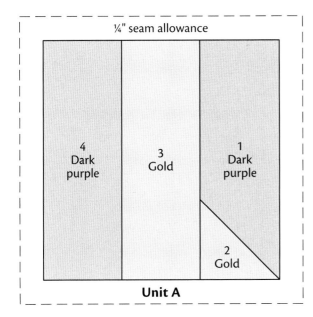

¼" seam allowance

| 4 Dark purple | 3 Gold | 1 Dark purple |
| 2 Gold |

Unit A

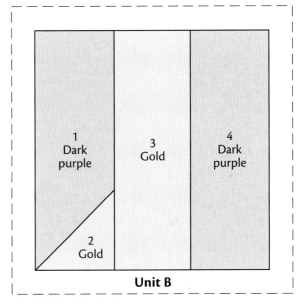

| 1 Dark purple | 3 Gold | 4 Dark purple |
| 2 Gold |

Unit B

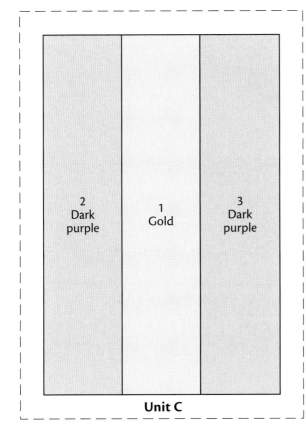

| 2 Dark purple | 1 Gold | 3 Dark purple |

Unit C

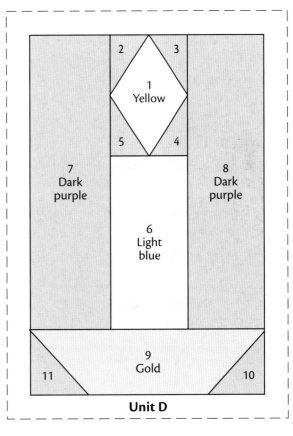

2   3
1 Yellow
5   4

7 Dark purple
6 Light blue
8 Dark purple

11
9 Gold
10

Unit D

Galaxy

Finished Quilt: 64½" x 92½"
Finished Blocks: 14"

Materials

- Assorted prints, ¼ yard *each* of 48 fabrics, including red, gold, orange, green, aqua, and purple, for blocks
- Dark blue tone-on-tone fabric, 6 yards for blocks and inner border
- Dark blue print, 2⅞ yards for outer border and binding
- Medium blue print, 2⅜ yards for blocks
- Backing, 6 yards
- Batting, 72" x 100"

Note: Although yardage amounts for foundation piecing are adequate, you may need more if you cut very generous pieces.

Cutting

The appliqué circle pattern is on page 83. For detailed instructions, refer to "Making Plastic Templates" on page 91, as needed.

From 24 of the assorted prints, cut:
    1 circle (24 total)

From the *lengthwise* grain of the dark blue tone-on-tone fabric, cut:
    2 inner-border strips, 1½" x 89"
    2 inner-border strips, 1½" x 61"

From the *lengthwise* grain of the dark blue print, cut:
    2 outer-border strips, 3½" x 95"
    2 outer-border strips, 3½" x 67"
    4 binding strips, 2¼" x 83"

Making the Blocks

Each block uses a different pair of assorted prints, while the medium blue and dark blue tone-on-tone pieces are the same in all of the blocks. Refer to "Foundation-Piecing Basics" on page 86 for detailed instructions as needed.

1. Make 96 copies each of the foundation patterns on pages 84 and 85. Each block is made from four of unit A and four of unit B.

Designed by Joyce Robinson; made by Penny Wolf

2. Paper piece the units in numerical order in the colors indicated on the pattern. Press and trim after adding each piece.

3. Sew coordinating A and B units together to make a quadrant. Repeat to make four matching quadrants. Sew the quadrants together as shown to complete the block. Repeat to make 24 blocks.

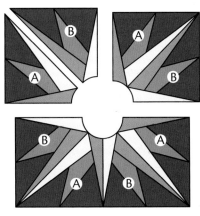

Make 24.

4. Prepare the circles for turned-edge appliqué and appliqué a circle in the center of each block.

Appliqué placement

Assembling the Quilt Top

1. Sew four blocks together to make a row. Press the seam allowances in one direction. Repeat to make six rows.

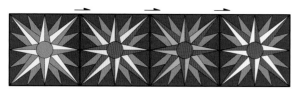

Make 6.

2. Sew the rows together and press the seam allowances in one direction.

3. Matching the centers, join the corresponding inner- and outer-border strips to make four border units.

Make 4.

4. Referring to "Mitered Borders" on page 93, sew the border units to the quilt and miter the corners. Trim the seam allowances to ¼" and press them open. Carefully remove the paper foundations.

Quilting and Finishing

1. Layer and baste together the backing, batting, and quilt top.

2. The quilt shown is quilted in the ditch, with the block seam lines quilted first, and then the other seam lines. The borders are also quilted in the ditch, as shown in the quilting suggestion below.

3. Bind the quilt using the 2¼"-wide dark blue strips.

Quilting Suggestion

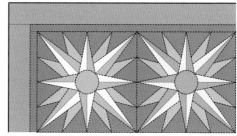

Young Expression

Aqua, brown, and white give this pattern a crisp, fresh, modern look. The visual texture in the flowered fabric creates a visual explosion in each block.

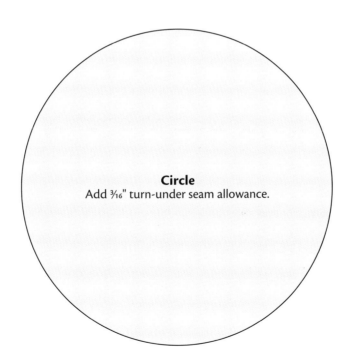

Circle
Add ³⁄₁₆" turn-under seam allowance.

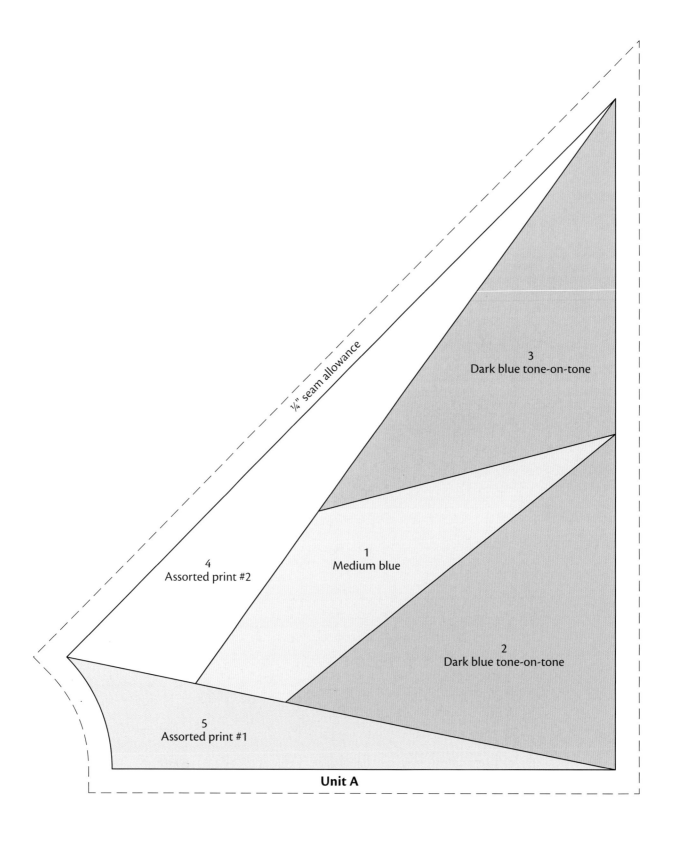

¼" seam allowance

3
Dark blue tone-on-tone

1
Medium blue

4
Assorted print #2

2
Dark blue tone-on-tone

5
Assorted print #1

Unit A

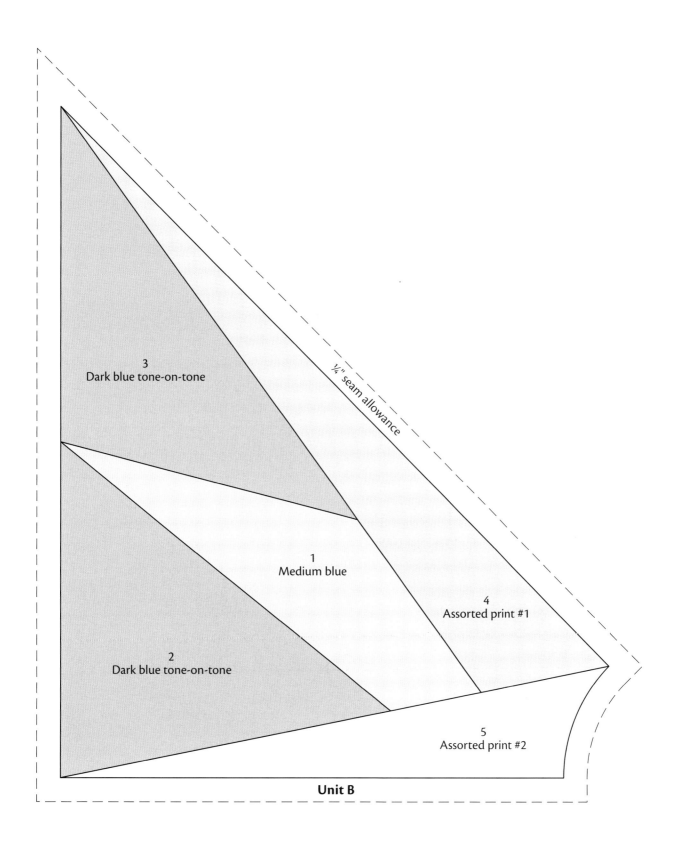

3
Dark blue tone-on-tone

¼" seam allowance

1
Medium blue

4
Assorted print #1

2
Dark blue tone-on-tone

5
Assorted print #2

Unit B

Foundation-Piecing Basics

Early quiltmakers sewed patches to muslin, to scraps of paper, and even to newspapers, because foundations added stability and accuracy. Today, most foundations are made from paper with the printed pattern on one side; scraps of fabric are sewn by machine in numerical order on the unprinted side of the foundation.

This method makes some difficult blocks easy to piece. No templates or rotary-cut pieces are required to sew accurate points and intricate designs. With a little practice and by following a few guidelines, you can create stunning quilts that look like only an expert could have pieced them. Let's get started.

Making Copies

First make copies of the foundation pattern; you'll need one foundation for each block or unit you intend to sew.

Materials appropriate for paper foundations include tracing, copy-machine, onion-skin, vellum, tissue, and parchment paper. Also available are laser-printer papers made specifically for reproducing foundations for this technique. Check quilt shops and office-supply stores for these options.

Many methods are available to reproduce foundations. Some methods are more accurate than others, and some are more expensive. Experiment to decide which one is right for your needs.

• Trace the foundation pattern directly onto tracing or other transparent paper and repeat to make the needed number of foundations.

• Use a photocopy machine to duplicate the foundation pattern. Always test for accuracy by first making one copy, and then comparing it with the original over a light source. If the copy differs more than 1/16", use another photocopier.

• Using a computer, scan the foundation pattern, and then print copies from a computer printer. As with the photocopier, check for accuracy.

• Make copies with your unthreaded sewing machine as described in "Making Needlepunched Foundations" below.

Making Needlepunched Foundations

Make one photocopy of each foundation pattern, and then layer it on top of several sheets of plain paper. Pin or staple the layers together in a few places, well away from the stitching lines.

With no thread in your sewing-machine needle or bobbin, machine stitch along each seam line on the foundation pattern. This will punch holes into the layers of paper, giving you a clear stitching line as well as perforating your foundation. When it's time to remove the paper, you can tear it away easily because the lines will have been stitched through twice.

To avoid any confusion about which fabric goes where, use a pencil or permanent marker to write the piecing order or color on each foundation.

Getting Set Up

Take a moment to prepare your machine and work space for the best results.

Set your machine stitch length to 18 to 20 stitches to the inch (1.5 mm). Choose a needle that's appropriate for the fabric you're sewing. See the tip "Use the Right Needle—and Stitch Length" on page 88 for guidance.

If you have one, use an open-toe presser foot for best visibility.

Choose a thread that blends with most of the fabrics; light tan or gray is ideal for almost all piecing.

Place an ironing board and iron within reach so you can easily press after sewing each piece. Or, you can use a pressing tool or your fingernail.

Finally, have a lamp or a sunny window nearby so you can see the piece size and placement of pieces through the paper foundation.

Fabric Preparation

Many quiltmakers like to cut fabric pieces before starting to sew, while others like the cut-as-you-go method—either way is fine. These suggestions will help you guesstimate the piece size and avoid wasted fabric.

For each foundation piece, add about ½" to each side when cutting out the approximate shape. Some shapes that are sewn at odd angles may require even more fabric. For those pieces that lie along the edge of the foundation, be sure that the fabric extends beyond the outer line, plus a little extra for trimming after the foundation is completed.

Make an extra copy of the foundation and cut out each paper piece. Use these templates as a guide for cutting fabric pieces.

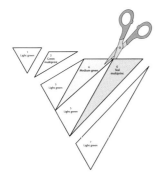

For long, skinny patches such as those in "Palm Star" (page 21), cut strips of fabric at least ¾" wider than the finished patch size.

Foundation Piecing

Now you're ready to foundation piece.

1. Place fabric piece 1 right side up on the unprinted side of the foundation. Hold the foundation and fabric piece up to the light to see if the fabric covers area 1 on the foundation, plus at least ¼" seam allowance on all sides. From the paper side, pin fabric piece 1 in place through the center.

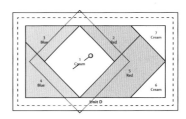

2. Turn the foundation over, fabric side up; using a piece of fabric sufficient to cover area 2 and its seam allowances, position piece 2 right sides together on piece 1. Both fabrics should extend at least ¼" beyond the seam line between areas 1 and 2. Holding the layers along this seam line, flip fabric piece 2 over to see if it's large enough to cover area 2, plus extra for the seam allowance. If not, either readjust the fabric placement or cut another piece and check again.

3. Holding the layers in place, turn the foundation over so the paper side is facing up. Carefully slide the layers under the presser foot and lower the foot; begin sewing at least ¼" before the start

of the printed seam line. Sew on the line and ¼"
beyond the end of the line.

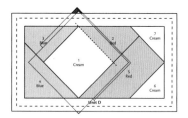

4. Remove the foundation from the machine and
   clip the threads. Fold the paper back on the
   just-sewn line and trim the extra fabric ¼" from
   the fold. You can use scissors to cut the seam
   allowances by eye or use rotary-cutting tools for
   trimming.

5. Turn the foundation over, open the just-sewn
   piece to be right side out and press the layers flat.
   If you're using an iron, use a dry one. Steam may
   warp or distort the foundation.

6. Repeat these steps to add piece 3 and the
   remaining pieces in numerical order until you've
   completed the foundation. Do not stitch along
   the outer seam line. Use a rotary cutter and ruler
   to trim the excess fabric and paper ¼" from the
   outer seam line of the foundation, creating a
   seam allowance.

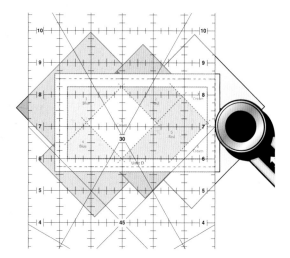

Joining Units

To join foundation-pieced units, use a walking
foot and sew them together with a scant ¼" seam
allowance.

1. From the paper side, at one corner, place a pin all
   the way through one foundation to the pin head.
   With right sides together, insert the pin in the
   corner of the adjoining unit, and then check to
   see if the point comes out exactly in the adjacent
   corner on the foundation. Reinsert if necessary.
   Repeat at the opposite end of the seam line and
   several places along the line.

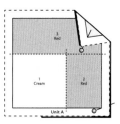

2. Keeping these pins in place, pin the foundations together, and then remove the first set of pins. Use silk pins if you have them; their thin shafts work well to keep the layers from shifting.

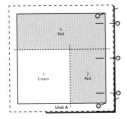

3. Sew the units together, removing the pins as you approach them.

4. When adding joined units to another unit as you would in "From My Garden" (below) and "Bow-dacious" (at right), remove the paper in the seam allowances before sewing the units together.

From My Garden

More Tips for Success

After joining foundation-pieced units or blocks, press the seam allowances open to reduce bulk.

If you can't trim the seam allowances because of crossed seams, lift the seam allowances away from the paper and then trim.

Iron delicate and non-cotton fabrics from the paper side.

Protect your ironing board from possible ink transfer with a pressing cloth.

To correct a sewing mistake, first stabilize the foundation by placing clear tape on the paper over the printed seam line you wish to resew. Then pulling the sewn layers apart, carefully cut the threads.

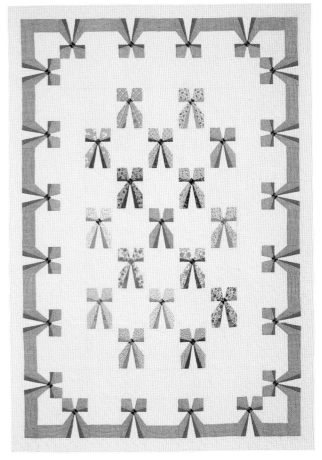

Bow-dacious

Basic Quiltmaking Lessons

We recommend that you read all of the instructions before starting a project, and that you cut and sew one block before cutting all of your fabric.

Use a rotary cutter, mat, and an acrylic ruler to cut the shape to the size indicated in the cutting list. The patterns list finished block sizes, which are typically ½" smaller than unfinished block sizes because they do not include seam allowances.

Basic Quilting Supplies

- Rotary cutter and mat
- Acrylic ruler: Many shapes and sizes are available; a good one to start with is 6" x 24" with ¼" and ⅛" markings.
- Scissors: separate pairs for paper and fabric
- Sewing machine
- ¼" presser foot
- Walking foot
- Darning foot
- Pins
- Ironing board and iron
- Marking tools (pencils, markers, etc.)
- Needles
- Thimble
- Safety pins
- Template plastic
- Thread

Preparing Your Fabric

We recommend that you prewash your fabrics. A shrinkage factor is included in our yardage computations.

Cutting

Measure, mark, and cut the binding and border strips before cutting pieces from the same fabric. Cut larger pieces before cutting smaller ones. For best use of the fabric, arrange pieces with cutting lines close or touching.

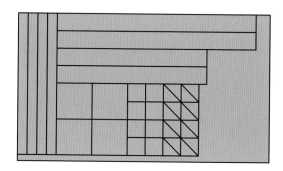

One or more straight sides of the piece should follow the lengthwise (parallel to the selvages) or crosswise (perpendicular to the selvages) grain of the fabric, especially the sides that will be on the outside edges of the quilt block. We indicate lengthwise or crosswise grain with an arrow on the pattern piece, if appropriate.

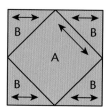

To find the grain line of your fabric for rotary cutting, hold the fabric with selvages parallel in front of you. Keeping the selvages together, slide the edge closest to you to one side or the other until the fabric hangs straight, without wrinkles or folds. Then lay the fabric down on your cutting mat and cut perpendicular to the fold line. Use this cut edge as your straight-of-grain line.

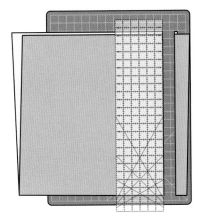

Many pieces can be cut from strips of fabric by rotary cutting. First, cut a strip of fabric the width needed. Then, crosscut the strip into pieces the required size.

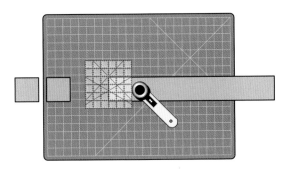

To cut from a template, place the template face down on the wrong side of the fabric and trace with a sharp pencil. Reverse templates should be placed face up on the wrong side of the fabric before tracing.

Machine Piecing

If the presser foot is ¼" wide, align the cut edges of fabric with the edge of the presser foot. If the presser foot is not the correct size, place masking tape on the throat plate of your machine ¼" from the needle to use as a guide.

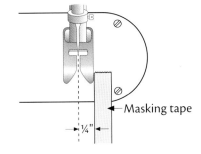

←— Masking tape

¼"

Making Plastic Templates

To make templates for machine piecing, trace the patterns provided onto template plastic with a fine-tipped, permanent-ink pen, making sure to trace the lines exactly. Mark the fabric grain line as shown on the pattern. Use utility scissors to cut out the templates, cutting exactly on the drawn lines. When placing the templates on the fabrics, pay careful attention to the grain lines noted on each template.

Pressing

Press all seam allowances to one side, usually toward the darker fabric, unless otherwise instructed. When joining blocks and/or rows, seam allowances are pressed to allow seams to nest, which reduces bulk in the quilt top.

Appliqué

Turn-under seam allowances are not included on appliqué patterns.

Using a light table, if needed, position background fabric over the appliqué placement diagram and lightly mark the major shapes with pencil or chalk. Or, finger-press the fabric in half lengthwise, crosswise, and diagonally to establish placement guidelines for the appliqué pieces.

Use a stabilizer on the back to support machine stitching that is dense (like satin stitching) and to keep the fabric from tunneling. Choose a stabilizer that matches the weight of the fabric. After the appliqué is complete, gently remove the stabilizer.

Turned-Edge Appliqué

It's helpful to have as many bias edges as possible on the perimeter of your appliqué pieces. Trace the seam line of the pattern onto template plastic; then cut on the traced line to make a template. Place the template face up on the right side of the fabric (face down on the right side for a reverse piece) and lightly draw around the template. Cut out each piece, adding a ³⁄₁₆" seam allowance outside the marked line.

On inside curves, clip the seam allowances almost to the marked seam line. Turn under the seam allowance and finger-press.

Pin or baste appliqué pieces onto the background fabric. To appliqué by hand, use a blind stitch and a thread color that matches the appliqué piece. To appliqué by machine, use a small zigzag or blind hem stitch and a matching or invisible thread.

If the background fabric shows through the appliquéd piece, carefully cut away the background fabric to within ³⁄₁₆" of the appliqué piece, or use two layers of appliqué fabric.

Fusible Appliqué

Raw-edge appliqué using paper-backed fusible web is a fast and easy way to appliqué. Because appliqué pieces are drawn on the paper side of the web and then flipped when ironed on the fabric, you may need to reverse some of the appliqué patterns. Add a ³⁄₁₆" seam allowance to those edges that lie under others.

Trace the pattern pieces, also drawing the needed seam allowances, onto the paper side of fusible web, leaving at least ½" between all of the pieces. Cut out the pieces, about ³⁄₁₆" outside each drawn line.

To eliminate stiffness, for pieces larger than 1", cut out the center of the fusible web ¼" *inside* the drawn line, making a ring of fusible web.

Following the manufacturer's instructions, iron the web, paper side up, to the wrong side of the fabric. Cut out the shape exactly on the drawn line. Carefully pull away the paper backing. Fuse the pieces to the background where marked.

To finish the raw edges, satin stitch or blanket stitch with a colored thread, or zigzag or blind hem stitch using invisible thread.

Bias Strips

Bias strips are cut at a 45° angle to the straight of grain of the fabric. They're stretchy and therefore ideal for creating curved appliqué stems.

Make your first cut by aligning a 45° guideline on your acrylic ruler with the cut edge or selvage of your fabric. Use this new bias edge to cut strips the required width.

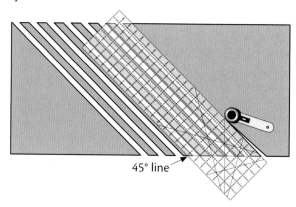

45° line

Prepare bias strips for appliqué by folding in half lengthwise, wrong sides together. Stitch ¼" from the raw edges. Position the seam allowances as shown and press them toward the center. Trim the seam allowances to ⅛".

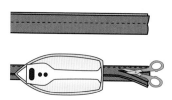

Squared Borders

Squared borders are added first to the sides of the quilt center, and then to the top and bottom. Lay the quilt top flat on a large table or the floor. Lay both side border strips down the vertical center of the quilt top and smooth carefully into place. Slip a small cutting mat under the quilt top (you'll need to do this at the top and the bottom edges) and use a rotary cutter and ruler to trim the border strips to the same length as the quilt top. Matching centers and ends, sew the border strips to the sides of the quilt top. Gently press the seam allowances away from the quilt center. Repeat this process along the horizontal center of the quilt top, including the just-added borders. Repeat for any remaining borders.

Mitered Borders

Mitered borders are added by sewing border strips to all sides of the quilt center and then mitering each corner. When joining each border strip to the quilt, begin and end stitching ¼" from the quilt-top corners, and backstitch. Referring to the diagrams, fold the quilt right sides together diagonally at one corner. Flip the seam allowances toward the quilt top, match seam lines, and pin through both layers about 3" from the corner. Place a ruler along the folded edge of the quilt top, intersecting the final stitch in the border seam line and extending across the border strip.

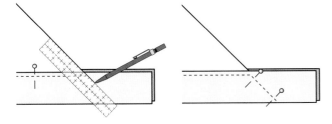

Draw a line from the seam line to the outer edge of the border as shown. Pin the layers together along the marked line. Starting at the inside edge with a backstitch, sew along the line to the outer edge of the border. Trim the seam allowances to ¼" and press them open. Repeat for all corners.

Marking Quilting Designs

Trace the quilting motif onto tracing paper. Place the tracing paper under the quilt top with a light source behind. Lightly mark the design on the quilt top with a hard lead pencil or a marker of your choice. Test any marking product for removability before using it on your quilt.

Straight lines may be marked as you quilt by using masking tape that is removed after quilting along its edge.

Backing and Basting

Make the quilt backing 4" to 8" larger than the quilt top. Remove the selvages to avoid puckers. Usually two or three lengths must be sewn together. Press the seam allowances open. Place the backing wrong side up on a flat surface, stretch slightly, and tape or pin it in place. Smooth the batting over the backing. Center the quilt top right side up on top of the batting. Pin the layers as necessary to secure them while basting.

Basting for Machine Quilting

Machine-quilted tops can be basted with rustproof safety pins. Begin at the center and place pins 3" to 4" apart, avoiding lines to be quilted.

Basting for Hand Quilting

Beginning in the center of the quilt, baste horizontal and vertical lines 4" to 6" apart.

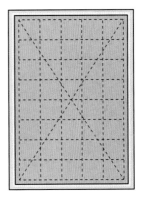

Quilting

Quilting in the ditch refers to quilting right next to the seam line on the side without seam allowances. Outline quilting refers to quilting ¼" from the seam line.

Machine Quilting

Before machine quilting, bring the bobbin thread to the top of the quilt so it doesn't get caught as you quilt. To do this, lower the presser foot, hold the top thread, and take one stitch down and up; lift the presser foot to release the thread tension and tug on the top thread to draw a loop of the bobbin thread to the top of the quilt. Pull the bobbin thread to the top. Lower the needle into the same hole created by the initial stitch, lower your presser foot, and start quilting. A walking foot is used for straight-line or ditch quilting. To free-motion quilt, drop (or cover) your feed dogs and use a darning foot. Start and end your quilting lines with ¼" of very short stitches to secure.

Hand Quilting

Hand quilting is done in a short running stitch with a single strand of thread that goes through all three layers.

Use a short needle (8 or 9 Between) with about 18" of thread. Make a small knot in the thread and take a long first stitch (about 1") through the quilt top and batting only, coming up where the quilting will begin. Tug on the thread to pull the knotted end between the layers. Take short, even stitches that are the same size on the top and back of the quilt. Push the needle with a thimble on your middle finger; guide the fabric in front of the needle with the thumb of one hand above the quilt and with the middle finger of your other hand under the quilt.

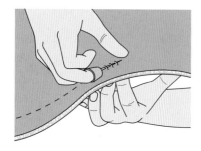

To end a line of quilting, make a small knot in the thread close to the quilt top, push the needle through the top and batting only, and bring it to the surface about 1" away. Tug the thread until the knot

pulls through the quilt top, burying the knot in the batting. Clip the thread close to the surface of the quilt.

Binding

Baste around the quilt about ³⁄₁₆" from the outer edges. Trim the batting and backing ¼" beyond the edge of the quilt top.

1. To prepare the binding strips, place the ends of two binding strips perpendicular to each other, right sides together. Stitch diagonally as shown and trim the seam allowances to ¼". In this way, join all the strips and press the seam allowances open.

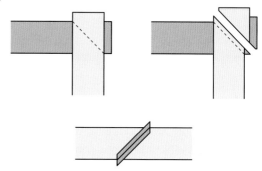

2. Cut the beginning of the binding strip at a 45° angle. Fold the binding strip in half lengthwise, wrong sides together, and press.

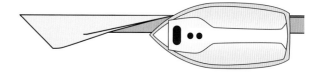

3. Starting in the middle of a side and leaving a 6" tail of binding loose, align the raw edges of the binding with the edge of the quilt top. Begin sewing the binding to the quilt using a ¼" seam allowance. Stop ¼" from the first corner and backstitch. Remove the needle from the quilt and cut the threads.

4. Fold the binding up, and then back down even with the edge of the quilt. Begin stitching ¼"

from the binding fold, backstitch to secure, and continue sewing. Repeat at all corners.

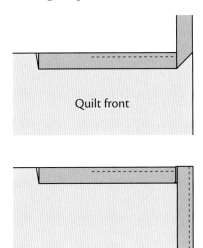

Quilt front

5. When nearing the starting point, leave at least 12" of the quilt edge unbound and a 10" to 12" binding tail. Smooth the beginning tail over the ending tail. Following the cut edge of the beginning tail, draw a line on the ending tail at a 45° angle. To add seam allowance, draw a cutting line ½" from the first line; make sure it guides you to cut the binding tail ½" *longer* than the first line. Cut on this second line.

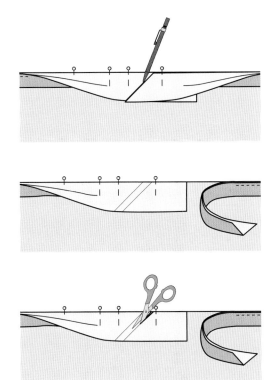

6. To join the ends, place them right sides together. Join the strips, offsetting them ¼" as shown. Press the seam allowances open. Press this section of binding in half, and then finish sewing it to the quilt. Trim away excess backing and batting *in the corners only* to eliminate bulk.

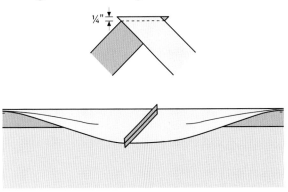

¼"

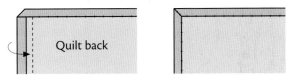

7. Fold the binding to the back of the quilt, enclosing the extra batting and backing. Blindstitch the fold of the binding to the back of the quilt, covering the line of machine stitching.

Quilt back

Hanging Sleeve

Sleeve edges can be caught in the seam when you sew the binding to the quilt. Cut and join enough 9"-wide strips of fabric to equal the width of the quilt. Hem the short ends of the sleeve by folding under ½", pressing, and then folding and pressing once more; topstitch close to the edge of the hem. Fold the sleeve in half lengthwise, wrong sides together, matching raw edges. Center the sleeve on the back and top of the quilt and baste. Sew the binding to the quilt. Once the binding has been sewn, smooth the sleeve against the backing and blindstitch along the bottom and the ends of the sleeve, catching some of the batting in the stitches.

You might enjoy these other fine titles from
MARTINGALE & COMPANY

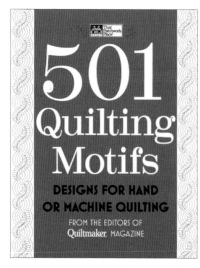

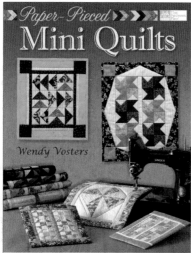

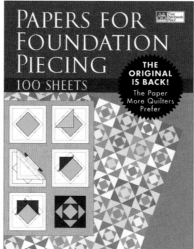

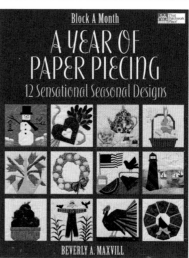

Our books are available at bookstores and your favorite craft, fabric, and yarn retailers.
Visit us at www.martingale-pub.com or contact us at:

1-800-426-3126
International: 1-425-483-3313
Fax: 1-425-486-7596
Email: Info@martingale-pub.com

America's Best-Loved Craft & Hobby Books®
America's Best-Loved Knitting Books®

America's Best-Loved Quiting Books®